70TH ANNIVERSARY COMMEMORATION EDITION

AMERICA'S WORST AVIATION DISASTER IN AUSTRALIA

Robert S. Cutler

Foreword by Amb. Kim C. Beazley

First published as *Mackay's Flying Fortress: The Story of Australia's Worst Air Crash in World War II* in 2003 by Central Queensland University Press

Revised edition published as *Australia's Worst Aviation Disaster* in 2014 Australia and *America's Worst Aviation Disaster in Australia* in the United States of America.

National Library of Australia Cataloguing-in-Publication entry

Author:	Cutler, Robert S., 1933- author.
Title:	America's worst aviation disaster in Australia / Robert Cutler.
ISBN:	9781925046694 (paperback)
Subjects:	United States. Air Force--History.
	Aircraft accidents--Queensland--Bakers Creek.
	B-17 bomber--Accidents--Queensland--Bakers Creek.
	Airplanes, Military--Accidents--Queensland--Bakers Creek.
	World War, 1939-1945--Aerial operations, American.
Dewey Number:	940.544973

Typeset in 12 point Garamond by Jane Dorrington

Disclaimer:
The opinions and conclusions expressed in this book are those of the author and the other individuals identified, and do not necessarily reflect the views of the US Air Force, the Royal Australian Air Force, the Mackay City Council, or any other governmental agency.

Printed and bound by Watson Ferguson & Company, Salisbury, Brisbane, Australia.

Courtesy Noel Tunny collection

Lt James T. Connally leads his crew from Flying Fortress number 40-2062 at Batchelor Field after the first bombing raid out of Australia by the19th Bomb Group. The aircraft was one of nine B17C Fortresses that staged through Del Monte on Mindanao, Philippines, to bomb the Japanese landing at Davao Bay. The results were not significant. Connally later became commander of the 19th bomb Group for a short time at Longreach in Queensland. James Connally Air Force Base in Texas is named in his honor.

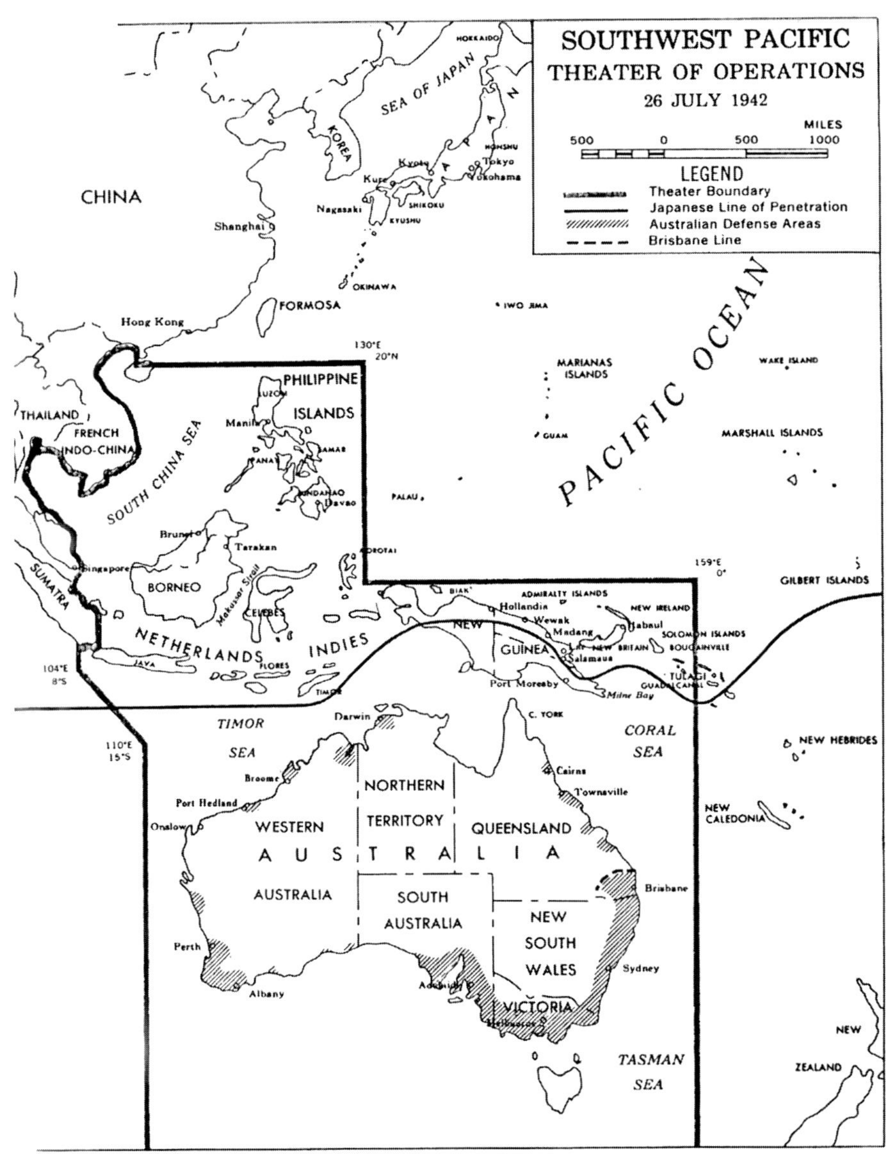

Map of Southwest Pacific area - 1942

Dedication

In memory of my father,
Samuel L. Cutler,
and the forty-one American servicemen he put aboard
Flying Fortress (VH-CBA) at Mackay Airport on June 14, 1943.

Acknowledgements

I want to acknowledge colleagues Colin E. Benson, in Australia, and Teddy W. Hanks, in America, for their extraordinary efforts during the past twenty years devoted to the Bakers Creek Memorial. This book would not have been possible without them.

I must express my sincere gratitude to Herbert S. Brownstein of the Smithsonian Air & Space Museum and author of *The Swoose: Odyssey of a B-17*, for generously sharing his research on the early wartime history of B-17C (40-2072) and his unpublished report on the Bakers Creek crash. They were valuable references.

My deep appreciation to Dale A. Adams, author of *The Souvenir*, and to Terry Hayes, local history reporter for *The Daily Mercury*, for generously contributing some of their thoughtful words.

Special thanks to retired USAF Lt. Gen. John 'Skip' Hall, Jr., a former commander of the US Fifth Air Force, who was instrumental in gaining official Air Force recognition for the Memorial, and to his successors, Lt. Gen. Paul V. Hester and Lt. Gen. Thomas C. Waskow, who became personally involved in the project. And also to Lt. Col. (Ret.) Eugene D. Rossel, Air Commandos Association, Senator Arlen Spector (PA) and Rep. Gary E. Miller (CA), for in bringing the Bakers Creek story to attention of the US Congress.

To Prof. David Myers ('ole Silvertail'), founding publisher of the CQU Press, who has been a guiding light and insightful mentor and motivator, and to Jack Neufeld, editor of *Air Power History*, who read early drafts of the manuscript and provided valuable comments.

Thanks also to the staffs of The George Washington University library and the Davis-Monthan AFB library, for locating many of the research sources, to the University of Arizona's Integrated Learning Center for technical assistance and the generous use of their 'world-class' computer facilities, and to the following individuals who contributed time to help make this book possible: Col. Timothy G. Murphy, Rod Manning, Reid Swift, Teresa LaRocco, Dr. George Benjamin, Morris Cobern, Paul Maynard, Mark J. Cutler, Romeo 'Connie' Costantine, Delmer L. Sparrowe, retired Lt. Col. H. James Greene, John Dolan, Elliet Aronson, Stuart A. Markson, and Paul Levenson, who read drafts of the manuscript and provided valuable comments and encouragement.

To David A. Fischer, airplane model guru and graphic artist, who generously gave valuable advice about the B-17Cs and designed the cover art for the book. And to the late, Jim Metzger, whose older brother, Marlin, was killed in the tragic Flying Fortress crash, and who built a website to promote communication among the crash victims' families [www.home.earthlink.net/~bakerscreek] to help tell the Bakers Creek story in America.

I wish to express sincere appreciation to Tom Brokaw, author of The Greatest Generation, who led me to refl ect upon a time I had almost forgotten. His recent book reminded me of the debt we owe "to those who came of age during the great depression and the Second World War -- those who gave us the world we have today." He opened my eyes to another group of Americans, those who did not return from the war, to whom we owe the deepest gratitude.

And to the families in Mackay who hosted the American servicemen on R&R leave from the New Guinea front when they were fi ghting side by side with Aussie Diggers against the invading Japanese.

Special thanks to Peter Frampton and John Cooper of Qantas Airways, Davis Brooks and Jennifer Pemberton of American Airlines, Rudy de Leon, of the Boeing Company, and to Wendell Holloway, Ed Fouhy, Heidi Berenson, Del Sparrowe and Mike Johnson for making it possible to build and deliver the bronze, scale model Flying Fortress replica to Mackay for the Bakers Creek Memorial.

Special thanks to the members of the Bakers Creek Memorial Committee, Col Benson, Brian Cuttriss, Jannette Thompson, John Pickup, and Cr Greg Thomsen, members of the Mackay City Council and the Mackay Returned Services League (RSL), for the fi nancial support from the Regional Arts Development Fund to publish the book. And to my wife Sarah, whose love, encouragement and tolerance have made all the difference in my life, and to our family, Mark, Debbie, Beth, Sally and Richard, and their children, so they may know the wider legacy of their Grandpa Sam's wartime diary. My dear sister, Joyce, gave me years of loving support for this project. Her family, Jennifer, Jane and Stephen, also who grew up with their grandfather, but without knowing the details of his wartime service in Australia.

I wish to acknowledge all of the errors and omissions as my own. Although much effort was made to locate the original sources of the wartime photographs used in this book, my sincere apology to those who may have been left out. If proper identifications can be made, the corrections will be included in a future edition.

Finally, when I was fi rst moved to write the original manuscript in September 1999, it was a labor of love. I did not anticipate the changes it would bring to my own life. It has been, simply, the most fulfi lling professional experience of my career and a deeply satisfying personal experience. I feel privileged to have the opportunity to share this nearly forgotten episode in the history of the Second World War in Australia with you.

RSC

Prelude

The young pilot, First Lieutenant Vern J. Gidcumb, sensed that the old B-17 seemed to labor more than usual during the takeoff, as if she were overloaded. Certainly it carried a full load with forty-one GI's packed tightly on board instead of the normal crew of six. Yet they wouldn't weigh nearly as much as a few good-sized bombs. Still, something wasn't right.

"Can't see a damn thing," his co-pilot complained a twinge of worry in his eager voice. "See anything?" It was just before daybreak and they had climbed into a fog layer almost as soon as the aircraft lifted from the run- way. Flight Officer William C. Erb hadn't flown this run with Vern before and there seemed to be something threatening about the sudden blackness.

"I'm not worried about that," Vern answered, "I'm on the clocks. But this turkey isn't pulling like it should, not nearly like it should." After another moment, "T'hell with this! I'm gonna take her back home."

"I'm gonna take her back home," Vern said. Indeed the old bomber had a name, Miss EMF. It meant "Miss Every Morning Fix-it," a fun name bestowed with cynical affection. Now the name seemed particularly ominous.

There was no more conversation. Within the next six minutes the Boeing B-17C Flying Fortress, operated by the 46th Troop Carrier Squadron, Fifth Air Force, plowed into the trees that lined a sugarcane field, five miles south of the Mackay Aerodrome, in North Queensland, Australia.

From: *The Souvenir*
by Dale A. Adams
Tucson, Arizona

Foreword

It has been 70 years since the B-17C Flying Fortress went down soon after takeoff from the Mackay Airdrome on 14 June 1943. During those many decades, much has changed. Slowly, through the efforts of people such as Professor Robert S. Cutler, Colin E. Benson, Teddy W. Hanks, Rod Manning, Ed Casey, Terry Hayes and others, the Bakers Creek crash story has emerged from the shadows of time.

With the second edition of this book, we learn the full story of the loss of forty American servicemen in a most unlikely scenario, and the remarkable efforts, both in Australia and in the United States, to remember them. Moreover, what follows could not be told when it happened due to wartime censorship, implications on American morale, and possible controversy concerning responsibility. We now have a clear accounting, as the incident takes its place in the history of World War II.

The book pays tribute to the lives lost that fateful day in 1943 and also affirms the friendship the people of Australia share with many Americans.

We in Australia are enormously grateful to the Armed Services of the United States of America for the close relationship they have extended to us for many years. The most significant component of that relationship, I believe, began during World War II when a million Americans went through Australia during that period — and Australia was threatened by enemy invasion.

It was during the beginning of the Pacific war that my nation experienced its darkest days. Many Australian inhabitants at the time believed the country would "fall" to the enemy. And the confidence that it would not was built to a large measure around the presences of the American servicemen, which began early in 1942 with the arrival of the American commander, General Douglas MacArthur. Historically, he is a bit of an ambivalent figure in the United States, but he is not in Australia. He was the commander of the Australian armed forces during the Pacific war, and prior to the Philippine Campaign, he had under his command 500,000 Australian and 200,000 Americans.

For much of the war, it was Macarthur's fight with Australian soldiers, but not with the people whose sacrifice we commemorate here. They were the Americans who came at once. They were the Americans who built confidence in Australia that we could survive, that we could resist. They were the Americans who made sure we could survive and resist by putting their own bodies on the line.

In the course of wars, most of the deaths that happen don't necessarily occur on the battlefield. Many deaths occur through illness, maybe illness picked up on the battlefield, but death also occurs elsewhere, and quite frankly, far too many by accident. A question often arises in the minds of some: "Is there a difference between one type of death than another?" The answer simply is, no, there is not. Not at all.

The men who perished at Bakers Creek were killed returning from a break – from a deployment, to a deployment — in a military aircraft. Their deaths in that deployment were every bit a contribution as the contribution of those American soldiers fighting in the approaches to Sanananda and Gona and Buna in the Papua New Guinea Campaign, of which they were a part.

The unique feature of this book, and the tragic accident it documents, is not simply the number of deaths, but rather, the extraordinary loss that occurred to so many American families, simultaneously. And how important it is that people in Australian and in American have ensured that this historic incident is remembered.

Lest we forget.

Kim C. Beazley, AC
Australian Ambassador
to the United States

Washington DC
June 14, 2013

Message from Mackay Regional Council

Twenty-one years ago, a permanent monument was erected by the citizens of Mackay honouring the sole survivor and the forty American servicemen who died in the Flying Fortress air crash at Bakers Creek during World War II.

This year marks the 70th anniversary of what we describe as "Australia's worst aviation disaster." In terms of loss of life, it proved to be the worst accident involving a transport aircraft in the Southwest Pacific war. These US Army troops were being returned to the jungle battlefields of New Guinea to help protect Australia from possible enemy invasion.

Wartime censorship restrictions at the time prevented local newspapers and radio stations from reporting the incident. Consequently, the accident was barely heard of outside of Queensland. However, thanks to a number of diligent people, the story of these young American servicemen lives on in our hearts and memories.

If not for people like Professor Bob Cutler from the United States, Mackay's RSL Historian, Col Benson, the members of the Bakers Creek Memorial Committee and others too many to name, the tragedy may well have gone unnoticed. Professor Cutler personally is connected to the incident. His late father, a US Army Air Corps officer, supervised the passengers loading and closed the door of the Flying Fortress aircraft that fateful day.

To mark the significance of the occasion, this special edition of the book, *Australia's Worst Aviation Disaster*, has been published. Originally launched at Mackay City Library on 13 June 2003, the book had been prepared to help provide closure for the family members of the crash victims. It now has been updated to include a set of photographs that were taken over the past ten years at memorial ceremonies held in Mackay and also in Washington DC.

I wish to make special mention of former Queensland Senator, the Honourable Santo Santoro of Brisbane. For more than a decade, Mr Santoro helped establish cordial relations between the Australian Ambassador and the American family members of the crash victims. It's people like him who keep the spirit of these servicemen alive through important annual remembrance efforts.

We remain grateful to the 40 American servicemen who lost their lives at Bakers Creek and to their families whose personal grief we have shared for 70 years.

Lest we forget.

Deirdre M. Comerford, Mayor
Mackay Regional Council

June 2013

Contents

Acknowledgements vi
Prelude viii
Foreword ix
Message from Mackay Regional Council xi
Introduction 1

Part I – "The Airplane"

1. Mackay, Australia – June 1943 5
2. The B-17C Flying Fortress 7
3. Birth of B-17C (40-2072) 9
4. The Transpacific Flight 12
5. Clark Field, The Philippines 14
6. New Home in Australia 19
7. Christmas Day Air Battle 20
8. Directorate for Air Transport 24
9. The Re-Christening 27
10. 317th Troop Carrier Group 29

End Notes 32

Part II – "The Air Crash"

11. The Final Flight 37
12. Assessment of the Calamity 44
13. Probable Causes of Crash 51
14. Conclusions 62

End Notes 65

Part III – "The Remembrance"

15. Mackay Remembers 71
16. Wartime Snapshot of Mackay 77

17. The List of Casualties 86
18. The Bakers Creek Memorial 90
19. A Simple Act of Remembrance 93
20. Letters to Family Relatives 95
21. Father Murf's Benediction 98
End Notes 101

Appendix 103
Bibliography 123
About the Author 125

* * *

Introduction

When I first visited Mackay in August 1999 to do research into the US Army Air Forces in Australia during the early part of World War II, I knew nothing about the Bakers Creek Memorial.

Armed only with a few handwritten pages in my father's wartime diary, describing a terrible plane crash involving a B17 Flying Fortress in 1943, when he was stationed here, my hope was to find out more about it. In fact, I was rather skeptical.

Ater interviewing a dozen or so local folks, including Terry Hayes, a newspaper reporter, Colin Benson, a local historian, and Rodney Manning, a former editor of *The Daily Mercury*, I was deeply impressed by their personal stories and, as one put it, "got caught up in the Bakers Creek story."

An article later appeared in the local newspaper providing much local history about the WW II B17 air crash and challenged me to find more information in America about the cause of the crash, matter of dark mystery among the locals for over fifty years.

Thus, for the past four years, I have become immersed in what is called, the Bakers Creek story; the history, facts, research, and remembrances of the worst aviation disaster in the Southwest Pacific war. The victims were 41 young American GIs in World War II; the heroes are the citizens of Mackay on the northeastern coast of Queensland. In this book, I shall attempt to do justice to their story and to the history and humanity of the people and places involved.

When I set out to write the Bakers Creek story, I was inspired by these people and by the realization that my job was to tell the story in America, despite its gaps and omissions. I was inspired by the work of these men and women. By writing their stories, I had found a way to say thank you. I wanted this book to be my gift to them, an expression of admiration and gratitude for what their families suffered and endured for seventy years, and for the legacy that could be passed on to future generations.

Most Americans know little of the wartime history of Australia, despite the fact that over 200,000 US troops were stationed there during World War II. Wartime security and censorship prevented reports of US troop movements in the Southwest Pacific.

This book recounts, in Part I, the early life of a B-17C Flying Fortress airplane that flew American troops between New Guinea and Mackay, in 1943, when the US Fifth Air Force ferried battle-weary troops from Port Moresby for R&R leave. Part II documents the plane's tragic crash on June 14, 1943 and presents a technical analysis of the possible causes of the crash. Part III describes the extraordinary action of the citizens of Mackay who commemorated the tragic WW II incident, some fifty years later, by building the Bakers Creek Memorial. My primary intention is to complement the work of the memorial.

It is not possible to go as deeply into other aspects of early aviation history in the SWPA as their importance might seem to warrant, and as many aviation buffs and political science scholars, no doubt, would expect. But the bibliography indicates where some of the issues can be studied further.

This book is a way of remembering more than the grim details of a forgotten WW II airplane crash near Mackay or preserving the memories of the American servicemen who died there. It is my hope to enable the Bakers Creek story to find its proper place in the history of World War II.

I am deeply indebted to the men and women whose stories you will find here, and to their families and friends who offered their comments and encouragement as well.

Robert S. Cutler
Washington, D.C.
June 14, 2013

Part I

THE AIRPLANE

Courtesy Sam Cutler collection

Queen Street, City of Mackay in 1943

1

Mackay, Australia — June 1943

In June 1943, as the Allies[1] were fighting to launch their first counter-offensive against the Japanese, the Japanese forces were advancing toward Australia through the jungles of Papua New Guinea. At the same time, a dark battle-worn bomber stood parked at the Royal Australian Air Force (RAAF) aerodrome near the tropical city of Mackay in Queensland. Mackay is 600 miles north of Brisbane on the northeastern coast of Australia.

Painted on its olive-drab fuselage were the white, five-pointed stars on blue background marking it as belonging to the US Army Air Forces. Unlike other AAF airplanes, however, there were no identifying serial numbers on its tail surfaces. Instead, displayed was the five-letter international civil registry code designating it as an Australian airplane VH-CBA.

Three miles north of where VH-CBA was parked is the city of Mackay. In this nineteenth month of war in the Southwest Pacific, Mackay was a popular, and safe, seaside resort. It was a city of wide streets, tropical gardens and long avenues of imported Royal Palms.

Courtesy Joyce A. Graham collection

American Red Cross Centre in Mackay 1943-44

In this peaceful grandeur, the US Army and the American Red Cross jointly operated a rest and recreation (R&R) center for the American soldiers assigned to war zone units located in the jungles and tropical swamps of New Guinea. From the combat outposts, the men were regularly airlifted on a four and a half-hour, non-stop flight from Port Moresby to Mackay, where they found refuge from the horrors of the battlefront and the hardships of life in the steamy, disease-ridden jungle.

As one of three converted bombers assigned to make daily R&R passenger runs between Mackay and Port Moresby, B-17C (VH-CBA) was poised to carry its cargo of servicemen north on their return. As it had done nearly every day for the past three months, the fully-serviced aircraft and its crew again stood ready again to transport some thirty five passengers back to the battlefields of New Guinea.

As the passengers filed through the single rear doorway of the large, converted bomber aircraft, they were directed to various locations in the former fighting machine. Some were directed to sit on the fitted plywood floor that now covered the windowless, noisy, drafty bomb bay. Others were allowed to occupy the Radio Operator's compartment, while still others simply sat on the wooden floor in the section aft of the radio compartment. The flight crew assigned to fly the airplane occupied the only seats equipped with body restraints. The passengers were to sit huddled in their confined space for the whole trip, leaving their places only to use the crude urinal relief tube located rearward near the tail wheel bulkhead.

A bystander watching the boarding process would quickly note that the airplane was a four-engine American Boeing B-17C Flying Fortress, but with Australian registry. There were obvious and important differences between this airplane and the newer B-17 models now operating in the Southwest Pacific and also over European battlefields.

She was an older C model, much worked, much tested and much loved.

B-17C Flying Fortress – 1941

2

The B-17C Flying Fortress

Unlike the newer B-17E, F, and G models, the older C-model Flying Fortress had a high dorsal tail structure. This rose abruptly from the rear of its fuselage, instead of the graceful "swooping-up" design, which characterized the later models. The C-model airplane was shorter than the newer B-17 variations. And there was no place in the empennage section for a tail gunner's position. The additional crew position was added to the later more familiar models, beginning with the B-17E.

The odd-looking aircraft was B-17C #40-2072, an American Flying Fortress bomber. Built by the Boeing Aircraft Company in October 1940, it was one of the second production run of 38 B-17s built then. And by June 1943, it was the oldest B-17C still operating in the Southwest Pacific Area — but no longer as a combat bomber. Stripped of its armor and armament, this obsolete warplane had been converted to an aerial transport. And from its many battle scars, it was evident the airplane had suffered much in the war that had been raging at the time for more than a year and a half.

While the B-17C was used in WW II for offensive bombing strikes, the B-17 bomber originally conceived in early 1931, was for a purely defensive mission: the protection of American coastlines from foreign surface fleets. It was this function, not its heavy armament that brought about its name — "Flying Fortress." [2]

An agreement was reached at the time between General Douglas Macarthur, then US Army Chief of Staff, and Admiral W.V. Pratt, Chief of Naval Operations:

> the Army air forces will be land based and employed as an element of the Army in carrying out its missions of defending the coasts, both in the homeland and in overseas possessions.

Through this arrangement, the Navy was assured freedom of action with no responsibility for coastal defense".[3]

When the United States entered the war in December 1941, the B-17C design was almost seven years old. And by 1943, four of the eight eventual B-17 models had been developed and would form the backbone of the USAAF bomber force in the Pacific, over Europe, and in North Africa. All told, some 12,731 of these B-17 aircraft would be built for service in World War II.

Over its life, the B-17 design evolved considerably. From its first prototype to the final "G"-series, the power of the B-17's engines increased by 60 percent; its cruising speed increased from 140 to 160 miles per hour; its fuel capacity grew from 1,700 to 3,630 gallons; its bomb load doubled from 4,800 to 9,600 pounds; and the length of the fuselage increased from almost 69 feet to nearly 75 feet.

The B-17 thus provided the performance breakthroughs that made it possible to implement the US Army Air Forces' theory of deep-penetration daylight bombing. It became the "guts and backbone of our worldwide air offensive", according to General H. H. Arnold, the commander of the Army Air Forces in 1942. With its highly accurate gyro-stabilized Norden bombsight and its capability of flying long distances (2500-mile range) at high altitudes, the B-17 Flying Fortress became America's first four-engine precision bombing platform.

The B-17C was an early model, but she did everything that was asked of her, and more.

3

Birth of B-17C (40-2072)

B-17C (40-2072), which ended up in Australia with the civilian designation VH-CBA, lacked many of the eventual B-17 enhancements. As part of the second 1940 production order for "thirty eight improved Boeing bomber aircraft", it was capable of carrying eight 600-pound bombs at a cruising speed of 230 mph over a range of 1,500 miles. And like other C-models, it was marked by a ventral gun emplacement in the lower fuselage that resembled a bathtub. Machine guns housed in the "bathtub" were operated by a kneeling gunner who could fire downward and to the rear to provide defensive coverage. There was no tail gunner position.

The plane was delivered to the US Army Air Corps at the Boeing factory in Seattle, WA, on October 31, 1940.[4] This B-17C was the thirtieth of a combined U.S.-British order for thirty eight airplanes of the same model. After the Lend-Lease Act[5] passed, the first twenty of these thirty eight Flying Fortresses were sent to England and became the first B-17s, in the spring of 1941, to fly in battle. However, these planes lacked the secret Norden bombsight and other improvements, such as controllable engine cowl flaps and self-sealing fuel tanks. The inability to regulate airflow around its nine cylinders often resulted in engine overheating during ground and low level flight operations.

As a result of the early Royal Air Force (RAF) battle experience, major changes were made in the subsequent series, called the B-17D. The changes came from lessons learned in actual combat by Fortress I, as the B-17C bombers of the Royal Air Force were known. As quickly as reports came in from US Army Air Corps advisors in England, many of the remaining B-17Cs were modified in the field.

The changes included: new, self-sealing fuel tanks installed in the wings; heavier armor and more of it, installed to protect the crew and vital systems (hydraulic, electrical, oxygen); the oxygen system was modified; intercom problems fixed; and new electrical systems put into the airplane.

However, there was one problem plaguing the British, which, since it never showed up on the American Fortresses sent to very high altitude, mystified the Boeing engineers and AAF specialists assigned to B-17 development. RAF crews had complained on enough occasions to make the matter alarming, that at high altitude the bomb-bay doors would jam. There never was a pattern to the jamming. Before takeoff the doors would cycle properly. Everything checked out. Then at high altitude with its subzero temperatures, the doors refused to open.

One Boeing engineer reported:

> We went out of our minds trying to get a fix on it, but we could never get the same kind of problem that seemed to be giving the British fits. Then by chance we talked with one of their [British] people who was assigned to England as a technical representative on the Fortress I. When he heard how the Americans were trying to solve the problem of the jamming bomb-bay doors, he stared at us in disbelief. Then he doubled up and roared with laughter.
>
> It turned out that the British had already solved their problem. You know what it was? It didn't have a damn thing to do with the Fortress or its electrical system or its bomb-bay doors. It seemed that while the airplane was climbing out to altitude the crewmen took the last-moment opportunity to relieve themselves. Some of them urinated into the bomb bay because there is a slight opening where the doors meet. And when the airplane climbed to where it was anywhere from 30 to 80 degrees below zero, you'd better believe those doors were frozen solid...[6]

Fortress (40-2072) was flown to the Sacramento Army Air Depot for upgrade modifications, reflecting the combat experience gained by the Royal Air Force against the Luftwaffe in Europe.

On June 13, 1941, per Aircraft Inventory Card, RBI-17C-40-2072, the airplane was transferred to Fort Douglas, near Salt Lake City, Utah, where it was assigned to the 7th Bombardment Group. Later that year, the airplane and its crew were assigned to the 19th Bombardment Group.

As political relations became strained between the United States and Japan in mid-1941, the USAAF Headquarters in Washington, DC believed the most likely area of attack was in the Philippines. The US defense forces in the Philippines left much to be desired. There were not enough bombers to provide the massive air support needed to defend the American and Philippine forces on the ground.

Air Force historians note:

> In late summer of 1941, the USAAF Headquarters made a decision to transfer the 19th Bombardment Group as permanent party to the Philippines. (In May 1941, the Group had ferried the first 21 B-17s to Hawaii). Now they were given "critical priority" in receiving new Fortresses as fast as they came off the production lines.
>
> But even that would take too much time. What about sending a provisional squadron to "fill in" in the Philippines until the 19th BG was fully equipped with the required number of bombers? The group then in the Hawaiian Islands was ordered to proceed as quickly as possible to their new assignment in the Far East. A massive effort was needed to sustain the unprecedented mission. There was no time to pioneer the route with one or two planes. It would have to be done with a large force and it must be done quickly. Operating under "utmost secrecy" the mission began. Australian officials offered full cooperation in preparing facilities at Rabaul in New Britain, at Port Moresby in New Guinea, and at Darwin in Australia. [7]

The 19th Bombardment Group was given a new mission: redeployment to the Philippines to supplement the limited forces defending the islands. The 19th Bomb Group's commander requested priority and received all of the available B-17Cs from the Sacramento Air Depot at McClellan Field in California. On October 1, 1941, B-17C (40-2072) joined the 19th Bombardment Group and was assigned to the 30[the] Bomb Squadron.[8]

4

The Transpacific Flight

The first element of nine B-17s to leave for their overseas assignment was the 30th Bombardment Squadron. On the evening of October 16, 1941, B-17C (40-2072) lifted its wheels from the US mainland and headed for the Hawaiian Islands, on the first leg of its 10,500-mile flight to reinforce American defenses in the Philippines.

On October 22nd, after spending five days in Hawaii and armed with twenty-five rounds of 50-caliber ammunition for each gun, the nine planes of the 30th Bombardment Squadron continued westward on its epic trans-Pacific flight. They followed the commercial air route used by the Pan American Clippers from 1933, bound for Manila. Refueling stops were made at Midway Island and at Wake Island.

The 14-hour leg (2,176 miles) from Wake Island to Port Moresby, New Guinea, was flown at night at an altitude of 26,000 feet, to avoid detection by Japanese forces reported to be active in the area.

Far beneath the nine Flying Fortresses, the Caroline Islands lay rich and green against the backdrop of the Southwest Pacific. Scattered clouds imparted a sense of height to the B-17 crews flying more than five miles above the earth. The bombers turned out all lights; maintaining complete radio silence over the islands. Bundled into fleece-lined flight suits and boots, clumsy in their goggles, leather helmets and oxygen-system hookups, the men scanned the skies about them with wary eyes. Deep as they were within Japanese South Pacific territory, the air had nevertheless so far been empty of enemy planes. It was a small miracle; they hoped it would remain. Even one American B-17 would be an inviting target to Japanese interceptors. Every minute without the expected sighting of enemy wings climbing to their altitude was another lease on life.[9]

From Port Moresby, the next hop was 934 miles to Batchelor Field, a Royal Australian Air Force (RAAF) base, 40 miles south of Darwin.

Finally, on November 2nd, just a month before the outbreak of the war, the nine B-17s of the 30th Bomb Squadron departed Batchelor Field for the 1700-mile leg to their new base at Clark Field, near Manila in the Philippines.[10]

It was a fateful move — war was not far away.

Map of the Philippines

5

Clark Field, The Philippines

When the 30th Bomb Squadron's B-17Cs arrived at Clark Field, this humid western-most US airfield was turf-covered and lay in open country, some 10,000 miles from California, and only 200 miles from the Japanese-occupied island of Formosa. By November 6, 1941, when other elements of the 19th Bombardment Group finally arrived, the Philippine Islands had the largest concentration of US Army Air Corps heavy bombers and fighter aircraft outside of the Western Hemisphere.

These new airplanes were the best available in America's limited pre-war arsenal. While no recorded nickname was assigned to B-17C (40-2072) when it was based in the Philippines, most of its sister planes had names. It was later called *Pamela* by the Fifth Air Force in Australia.[11]

War Comes to Clark Field

In the last days of November 1941, a single Japanese bomber began its nightly flights over Manila. On December 1, the 19th Bomb Group was informed that, despite the fact no air encounters with the Japanese had been reported, US Army personnel were to consider themselves at war with Japan.[12]

On Wednesday evening, December 3rd, orders were given to move sixteen of the 19th Bomb Group's Flying Fortresses some 600 miles south to a new airfield at the Del Monte pineapple plantation on the island of Mindanao. But the B-17s of the 30th Bomb Squadron, including 40-2072, remained at Clark Field continuing to fly training missions.

Early morning on December 8th (across the International Date Line from America, where it was December 7th), a Navy radio operator at Cavite Station, on Luzon Island, intercepted the message — "Air raid on Pearl Harbor".

Shortly after ten that morning, the 19th Bomb Group received a warning message that a Japanese force of 192 bombers was fast approaching Clark Field and was expected within the next 20 minutes.[13]

Following the necessary preflight preparations, fifteen B-17s took off to avoid being caught unprotected on the ground. For more than three hours, B-17C (40-2072) and her sister aircraft circled Mt. Arayat, flying in and out of cloudbanks, without seeing the attacking Japanese bombers.

The 15 Flying Fortresses returned to Clark Field just before noon. Upon landing, to expedite fueling, they lined up in straight lines along with some 50 P-40 fighter planes. The crews began servicing the aircraft and were ordered to stand by as food was delivered to them. The pilots and navigators had a hurried meal and reported to Group headquarters for a preflight mission briefing.

Shortly after noon on December 8, about 10 hours after the Japanese attack on Pearl Harbor, the men of the 19th Bomb Group, standing by their airplanes, heard a low whistling sound, resembling wind blowing through trees. The sound grew louder and louder as Japanese aircraft, in two formations, approached Clark Field from the west at 18,000 feet.

As the apex of the first formation approached, the bombs started falling. As the "V" widened, the area of bomb blasts widened. By the time the last of the 25 twin-engine Mitsubishi medium bombers (later code-named *Betty*) had passed, the second formation of 27 bombers started over the field.

The Japanese had caught the 15 B-17s parked on the ground. The American military commanders badly underestimated the airpower experience that the Japanese had gained while fighting in China. For example, following the initial bombing, 51 Zero fighters came in low and subjected the parked aircraft to repeated strafing attacks. The strafers proved to be more devastating than the high altitude bombers, as their bullets struck the fully fueled B-17s. [14]

The Japanese air attack on Clark Field lasted only 40 minutes. When the enemy airplanes withdrew; every B-17 at Clark Field was either damaged or destroyed. American air power in the Philippines had been effectively eliminated; parked on the ground without firing a shot. Of the 15 B-17s originally parked at Clark Field, only five remained standing, although damaged and unflyable. From these five airplanes, three were ultimately patched so they could be flown. Of these, the only one to fly again in combat was airplane 40-2072.

As reported by aviation historian, Martin Cadin:

> The men at Clark Field did their best to restore the smoking, gutted shambles to an operational air base. With many of the engineering and maintenance shops destroyed, trying to save the few airplanes left was a task demanding superhuman effort, the ability to work without sleep, and mechanical genius. Most hangers were gone, and the men worked out in the open, maddened by swarms of flies

> that settled thickly on the field. While the mechanics struggled to piece together three or four Fortresses, which might be able to fly, others sifted through the debris to restore communications and other vital operational facilities. The main runway was cratered and holed and littered with debris. The men filled in holes until they had a single runway about 2,000 feet in length. That was all. Beyond that one strip the pilots of the B-17s had to weave and dodge to avoid craters and huge chunks of concrete and metal.[15]

B-17C (40-2072) had not escaped unscathed. Damage from enemy machine-gun fire had penetrated her wings and fuselage. Miraculously, no significant damage was sustained to any of the aircraft's flight systems; the crew chief soon declared her flyable.

On December 10, 40-2072 once again was airborne on reconnaissance mission. In the company of another B-17, she flew over Lingayen Gulf where they were intercepted by five enemy aircraft. (American aircrew claims of enemy sightings were often divided by three, for reliability). They claimed to have destroyed one attacker and damaged the others. Both B-17s returned safely to Clark Field.[16]

Shortly after their return, however, the bomber pilots received orders to abandon Clark Field. Preparations were immediately began for their redeployment 600 mile south to the relative safety of Del Monte; the only American airfield in the Philippines not yet attacked by the Japanese. Takeoff on December 11 for that base was scheduled for just before dawn so they could pass out of range of attacking enemy aircraft by daybreak.[17]

As the four engines were being run up [ground tested], a gasoline leak was detected. The engines were shut down and on inspection, the leak was found to be in the fuel line that ran between an engine and the firewall. To stop the leak, the damaged fuel line would have had to be replaced with one from a wrecked B-17. The alternative was to tape over the leak and risk the possibility of fire in flight.

Since the replacement option would expose the airplane, its crew and passengers, to the danger of probable Japanese air attack during daylight, it was decided to take the risk of a temporary repair and get out of Clark Field during darkness. This turned out to be a fortunate choice; Clark was attacked again later that day while the wounded B-17 was making its way safely to Del Monte.[18]

Overloaded with men, equipment and spare parts needed to service the airplanes at Del Monte — and with the two experienced pilots, 1/Lt. "Red" Mueller and 1/Lt. Frank Kurtz, at the controls -- Flying Fortress 40-2072 again rose into the air, leaving behind the gross devastation on the ground at Clark Field.

Given the tactical situation at the time, preparations began for evacuating the B-17s from Del Monte to Australia, where they would no longer be within range of the fast advancing Japanese forces. To make the long overwater crossing, additional bomb bay fuel tanks would be needed and soon were airlifted from Clark Field.

One of the two bomb bay fuel tanks installed in 40-2072 was found to have been damaged by gunfire during the earlier attack on Clark Field. No sheet metal specialists could be found at Del Monte among the personnel thus far evacuated. The only known surviving sheet metal worker in the 19th Bomb Group, Corporal Leon Long of the 30th Bomb Squadron, was still on Luzon. Now assigned to an anti-aircraft battalion, he had been sent to the Bataan Peninsula where preparations were being made to accommodate the retreating American and Philippine forces.

In northeast Bataan, Corporal Leon J. Long of Sturgeon Bay, Wisconsin, had spent the day digging a gun emplacement. At dark, he crept under the floor of a native but to get out of the rain and get a few hours of badly needed sleep. Shortly before midnight, he heard someone calling his name, but he was too exhausted to respond. Soon, his sleep was violently disturbed by a kick to his bottom and the light of a flashlight shining into his eyes.[19]

Corporal Long had been tracked down by Sergeant Carl Schumaker, his Line Chief at Clark Field. Sgt. Schumaker told Long that he was needed at Del Monte to repair a bomb bay tank. The two climbed into a Jeep and sped back to Clark Field. Upon their arrival, the first task faced was locating Cpl. Long's toolbox. The Sergeant had buried all toolboxes to deny them to the invading enemy forces. Cpl. Long's box was found, and excavated. He and the box were rushed to the two waiting airplanes. They took off as soon as Long was onboard, about two hours after sunrise.

Though the flight was made during daylight, they arrived at Del Monte without encountering any enemy aircraft. Cpl. Long was quickly taken to where B-17 40-2072 was standing and shown the damage. The side of the aluminum bomb bay tank had been hit by gunfire. There was a hole near the tank top, about a foot in diameter. Since there was no aluminum sheeting available to close the hole, Corporal Long cut off the top of a steel drum. And using a damaged tire inner tube as a seal, he bolted the steel drum top to the tank, effectively patching the hole. Fortunately, he had an assortment of bolts in his toolbox, which were used to form a double row around the patch.[20]

The repaired tank was hoisted into the bomb bay and filled with 400 gallons of gasoline. A few drops seeped out of the patch, but the crew found it acceptable under the circumstances. The aircraft was then prepared for flight.

Shortly after Corporal Long finished the repairs, Mueller and Kurtz, in their Clark Field survivor, B-17C 40-2072, prepared to leave the Philippines for a new assignment at Batchelor Field, an RAAF airfield in Australia. Having spent the past week at Del Monte repairing their faithful airplane, they were ready for a nine-hour flight over open water to a new home.[21]

At two o'clock in the morning, December 11th, along with the other B-17s of the 19th Bombardment Group, they started engines and prepared to depart the beleaguered Philippines. Taxiing away from her muddy parking spot, the airplane came abruptly to a stop. One of the crew jumped out, ran back to where Cpl. Long stood watching the departure. Lt. "Red" Mueller, the pilot, sent word that since he fixed the tank that gave them the capability to make the flight to Australia, Cpl. Long was to bring his tool box and climb aboard.

Thus Cpl. Leon Long escaped the fate of other ground crew members who were left behind at Clark Field. They were required to join the infantry troops in the failed attempt to halt the invading Japanese forces. The tiny Bataan peninsula would ultimately become the temporary sanctuary for some 36,000 exhausted defenders. The starving troops on Bataan surrendered to the Japanese on April 9th. One month later, the battle for the Philippines ended. Many captives died during the forced and tortuous march to prison camps in northern Luzon.

It was a dark hour for the Allied Forces in the South West Pacific. Flying Fortress B-17 40-2072 was about to assume a new role in the war.

6

A New Home in Australia

Flying Fortress B-17 40-2072 arrived at Batchelor Field near Darwin on the evening of December 18, 1941. Lt. Red Mueller, his crew and passengers including the lucky Cpl. Long, arrived on Australian soil at 7:30 PM. It was the second time the airplane had landed at the dusty RAAF airfield that previously served as one of the refueling stops on her pre-war trans-Pacific flight, little more than one month earlier. Of the original 35 B-17s that made up America's bomber force in the Western Pacific in November 1941, only 14 survived to reach Australia.

From their new base in Australia, three B-17s, including 40-2072, were ordered to mount a combined bombing, re-supply/evacuation mission to Del Monte in the Philippines. From Batchelor Field, the airplanes were loaded with bombs to be dropped on the Japanese invasion forces at Davao, on the island of Mindanao, 70 miles from Del Monte. And after landing at Del Monte, the B-17s were immediately reloaded with bombs, serviced for the return trip, and made ready for a repeat attack on Davao, enroute back to Australia. Other B-17s loaded up with stranded American military and civilian personnel, evacuating them from the only operational airfield in the Philippines remaining in American hands.[22]

On December 19th, Japanese aircraft finally discovered the airfield at Del Monte and began making routine strafing attacks. The following day, Japanese sea borne forces landed at 22 places on Luzon Island. American air operations at Clark Field were suspended. All U.S. forces were evacuated by ground to Corregidore on December 24, although it was almost a week later before the enemy ground forces arrived.[23]

7

Christmas Day Air Battle

The zenith of B-17C 40-2072's wartime service came during its last combat flight. On December 24, 1941 the plane departed from Batchelor Field on what became a dramatic mission. The pilot, Lt. Mueller, was later quoted saying:

> Christmas of 1941 was sort of sad for our side. Our guys in the Philippines were taking an awful beating from the enemy and were due to receive even worse at Bataan and Corregidore.[24]

At 10:15 on that morning, December 24, 1941, 40-2072, the lone surviving bomber of the Japanese attack on Clark Field, and the last one of the 30th Bomb Squadron's original nine Flying Fortresses left Australia with two other B-17s for the long trip north to the enemy endangered field at Del Monte. The mission was to evacuate trapped personnel. The flight path took them near the Japanese invasion forces coming ashore at Davao, which threatened the airfield at Del Monte.[25]

Flying in darkness on a changing course to avoid detection, they arrived at 7:30 pm on the roughly repaired, bomb-damaged landing strip at Del Monte. No sooner had they switched off engines than the crews were ordered to cancel their plans to evacuate personnel. Instead, they were to takeoff on a combat mission to bomb the Japanese invasion forces coming ashore at Davao. Then they were to continue flying the 1500-mile return trip to Batchelor Field (Australia), as they had done on previous shuttle bombing runs. The three pilots were told to plan their own bombing attack.

Ground crews began the laborious task of pumping 2,100 gallons of high-octane gasoline into the fuel tanks from the only surviving refueling truck. Since the truck held only 800 gallons, three trips were needed to complete the job. The bomb bays of the three B-17s were then loaded with seven 300 lb.

bombs, arranged in one-half of the bomb bay. A droppable auxiliary fuel tank occupied the other half, to give the airplane the extra range required for the long overwater trip.[26]

Taxiing out for takeoff, one of the airplanes suffered a flat tire, had to delay departure until it could be fixed. The two remaining aircraft took off, as planned, in the early morning darkness at 4:30 am on Christmas Day, and climbed to a cruising altitude of 20,000 feet. With crews on oxygen, they approached the target.[27]

Heavy anti-aircraft fire was encountered near the bomb release point; 40-2072 was hit twice on the right wing. A large hole was opened near the tip and another, about the size of a barrel, just behind the inboard engine, which damaged the fuel feeder tank. It was feared the hits might also have damaged the main wing spar.[28]

In spite of the damage to 40-2072, the two aircraft completed their bombing run at 20,000 feet, as planned. Bombs were dropped on the enemy-held airfield at Davao. Parked fighters and bombers there could be seen exploding or set aflame. Some bombs struck a hangar.

During the Davao attack, the other B-17 had one of its four engines fail, slowing it down considerably. Clearing the target area, the pilot of 40-2072 reduced its power and elected to descend and fall into formation with the slower aircraft. By flying in formation, the guns of both Flying Fortresses could more effectively be used to defend each other from any possible enemy fighter attack.[29]

The two airplanes set a southeasterly course for open sea and the long trip back to Australia. Suddenly, one waist gunner reported ten enemy aircraft climbing toward them. The two B-17s climbed back to 20,000 ft. to avoid interception. However, the Japanese planes closed in on their prey and opened fire, which the B-17 crews answered.

For the next 40 minutes, the crews of the two Flying Fortresses were kept very busy. Two enemy airplanes dove for the blind spot in the B-17's defenses — the unarmed tail. To bring the attackers into range of his two waist gunners, Lt. Mueller, pilot of 40-2072, deliberately kicked the rudder pedals to make the airplane "fish-tail." As enemy aircraft continued their attacks, their gunfire punctured the bomb-bay fuel tank, cut aileron cables, knocked out controls for the engine turbo-superchargers, and finally hit the oxygen supply.

Without life-sustaining oxygen, the pilot of 40-2072 was forced to abandon the other B-17 at 20,000 feet, and make a hurried crash dive descent to a lower altitude, before all aboard lost consciousness from hypoxia. It was an extremely delicate maneuver, as the condition of the wing spar was not known. Had it suffered significant damage from the anti-aircraft burst at Davao, the wing could have failed if it was over-stressed by such sudden actions.[30]

Risking a failed wing, the pilot pushed the control column forward and put the airplane into a hasty, but controlled, rapid descent. The airspeed indicator registered 350 miles per hour, 30 mph over the "Red Line." (Maximum design airspeed marked on the airspeed indicator). The crew hung on to steady themselves.[31]

Afraid that he might lose the right wing at any moment, the pilot eased back on the control column, and the damaged airplane slowly pulled out of its rapid descent toward earth, finally leveling off at 4,000 feet. The wing tips seemed to bend a couple of feet, the rivets holding the skin to the wing spars had popped off for about eight feet. But the wing spars held. With two wounded crewmen onboard, the navigator set a course for the safety of Batchelor Field, 1100 miles away. Apparently the maneuver to take the airplane to a lower altitude by diving caused the enemy attackers to assume that they had destroyed the B-17. Japanese records claim the attackers "probably" shot it down.[32]

When visual contact with Batchelor Field was finally made, the plane's flight path was aligned with the 3,600-foot runway. As the wheels took hold in the red mud of the unpaved landing strip, the tail wheel settled down as the throttles were retarded to slow the airplane as it raced through sheets of water thrown up by the turning propellers. The plane came to a stop and the four overworked, nine-cylinder Wright Cyclone R-1820 engines shut down. At mid-afternoon on Christmas Day 1941, Lt. Mueller's crew left their airplane for the last time. Although it was the end of 40-2072's combat career, the badly damaged plane had returned her precious human cargo to safety, enabling them to fly and fight another day.

B-17C (40-2072) remained at Batchelor Field -- out of commission for repairs.[34] The pilot had brought the plane home with some 1,100 bullet and shrapnel holes in it. That number still stands as a record in the Pacific war.[35]

According to Colin E. Benson, Mackay RSL Historian, B-17C (40-2072) as a Flying Fortress bomber in the early part of the war (December 1941) had an extensive combat history.

> From its first combat mission on December 8, 1941 out of Clark Field in the Philippines, the airplane and crew sunk two loaded Japanese transports, a destroyer, and a submarine (using only one bomb, from 20,000 ft.), and shot down 21 planes, including a four-engine flying boat.
>
> It also bombed Japanese landing parties; enemy-occupied airdromes, and sustained two direct hits from anti-aircraft fire, while carrying over 100 machine-gun bullet holes.

> The aircraft evacuated 28 pilots from the Philippines at night and in a tropical storm, and escaped a devastating aerial fighter ambush, as the Japanese advanced across the Southwest Pacific toward New Guinea and Australia during late December 1941.[36]

The B-17C had performed heroically. It was badly hit, but it still had a further role to perform.

Courtesy Herbert S. Brownstein collection

Heavily mauled B-17C 40-2072 shown at Batchelor Field near Darwin, waiting for repairs to combat damage suffered during the Christmas Day 1941 mission. The aircraft participated in the attacks on Japanese landing parties in the Philippines and was hit over 1000 times. The plane had evacuated twenty eight pilots from Del Monte when the Philippines fell to the enemy — pilots who would not otherwise have been able to carry on the war against the Japanese.

8

Directorate for Air Transport

As the new year of 1942 began, the Japanese forces were moving fast down the south Pacific. The old, battle weary B-17C remained unserviceable at Batchelor Field. But Australia was soon to become the focal point for the combined Allied military operations in the Southwest Pacific.

Each of Australia's five mainland states had developed its own transportation system, but with no regard to its compatibility with those of its neighbors. Without uniform standard gauge tracks, their railways were built with different sizes, sometimes even within the same state. Highway systems were equally inadequate for military needs. Slow and hazardous water transport along Australia's eastern seacoast was not a viable alternative. Japanese submarines patrolled the north-south shipping lanes and sank many merchant vessels plying these waters.

The problems of land and sea transportation made air delivery of critical supplies the only reliable method of moving military cargo to the beleaguered forces in the island battle zones to the north, in Java, New Guinea and the Philippines. However, the US Army Air Forces in Australia (USAFIA) had not been authorized to have an air transport organization, by the War Department, and within the Australian RAAF, air transport was rare. While transport-type aircraft had been requested from the United States, the demands for combat aircraft prevented the delivery of aircraft uniquely designed to haul cargo.[37]

On January 28, 1942, Major General George H. Brett, the first commander of the U.S. Army Forces in Far East (USAFIA), directed that all combat airplanes unfit for combat be made part of a new directorate for air transport, within the Southwest Pacific Area (SWPA) "to overcome the immediate airlift shortage." [38] The new airlift command was established as an Australian-based

Allied organization, not to be confused with the USAAF Air Transport Command that later flew Pacific air routes to Australia.

As a result of that order, any airplane that could be made flyable was pressed into transport service. Some damaged combat airplanes were cannibalized for parts. Even the thin aluminum skin was removed from abandoned airplanes and used to patch holes in other airplanes. In some cases flattened metal from tin cans was used to patch smaller holes.

The big, damaged 40-2072 still sat on the ground at Batchelor Field. Yet despite critical damage to its wing and the large number of bullet holes in its skin, it was decided that she could be made flyable. Because of the shortage of available facilities and manpower, only repairs necessary to fly the airplane to another repair facility were made. This meant patching the large holes in the wing, repairing the hydraulic lines that activated the brakes, and doing relatively simple repairs to make the broken plane airworthy for just one more flight.[39]

Maintenance logs (Form 781-1) indicating the specific repairs made to 40-2072 have not yet been found, but a likely scenario can be hypothesized. The airplane probably was repaired temporarily with patches made over the holes in its wings, horizontal stabilizer and the rudder. Repair to the hydraulic system was limited to replacing a small section of metal tubing to make the brake system operational. The damaged control cables most likely were replaced as well. In this condition, and with its four engines operational, the airplane was flown 800 miles to Archerfield (in Brisbane) for more extensive repairs and removal of all of its heavy armament, for her conversion to transport duty.

The scenario is supported by a comment in General Brereton's diary.[40] He stated that one of the three B-17Cs at Batchelor Field was turned over for non-combat service when Air Transport Command in Australia was born.[41] The other two B-17s serial numbers were traced: aircraft 40-3062 went to Java 14 February 14, 1942 and 40-3091 was scrapped at Batchelor Field. The remaining B-17C, referred to in Brereton's diary, must have been 40-2072, last reported on the ground and out of commission because of damage she sustained over Davao — now the last B-17C operating in the Southwest Pacific.

At Archerfield Field, ground crews then worked two shifts daily to repair the damaged aircraft for transport duty. Spare parts were unobtainable, making it necessary to cannibalize or repair used parts. For example, when a new wing was needed for 40-2072, the damaged wing was removed and used as a pattern to design and install brackets that were then mounted to the underside of an available C-39 transport. The C-39 was then flown to Batchelor Field. One wing was removed from an abandoned B-17C, secured to the underside of the C-39 for its return flight to Archerfield, and then installed on 40-2072.[42]

The men restoring 40-2072 to transport flying status referred to her as *Old Unsinkable.* In March 1942, the renewed aircraft was listed as the only B-17C flying among the aircraft of the 22nd Troop Carrier Squadron. By April 1942, American *Newsweek* reporter, John Lardner, wrote of his encounter with the airplane, now fully restored to flying status. He commented that the airplane had been neatly patched and was now ready for operation.[43]

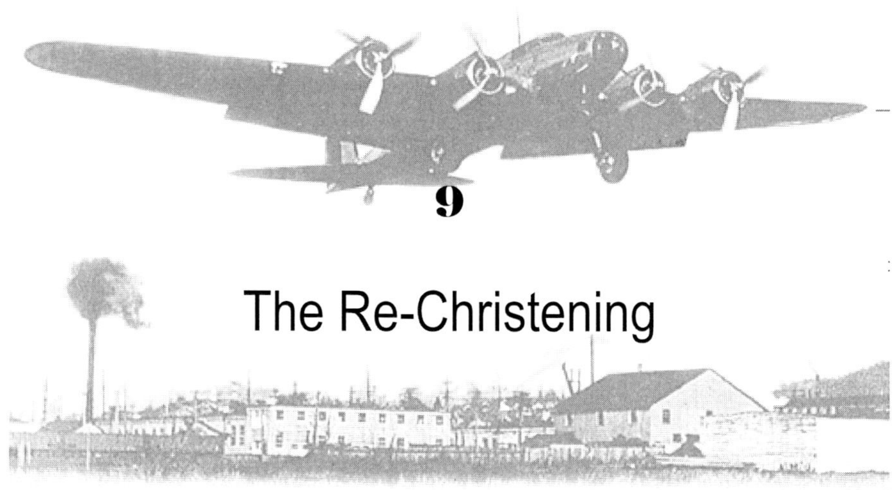

9

The Re-Christening

Early in 1942, the Directorate of Air Transport (DAT) of the Allied Air Forces was formed under RAAF (Australian) operational control. All US Army aircraft assigned to DAT, including our B-17C, were to display a five-letter Australian civil aircraft registration, instead of their Army Air Forces' serial numbers. The aircraft and crews remained attached to their US Army flying units. So when veteran B-17C (40-2072) returned to service as a transport, she carried the new designation, VH-CBA, and would carry that unique identifier in all future USAAF reports.[44]

Japanese air operations in the SWPA from March to July 1942 were leading to their planned amphibious assault to take Port Moresby.

According to historian Geoffrey Perret:

> This dusty, backwater town (Port Moresby) became the focus of a bitter struggle for control of New Guinea. Americans and Australians were hacking airfields out of surrounding bush wherever there was a well-drained, level area. Each field was named for its distance from the town. There was a Three-Mile Field, a Seven-Mile Field, and so on.
>
> The Japanese raided the airfields early every morning and late every afternoon. They also sent a couple of bombers after dark, to make sure nobody on the ground got a good night's sleep.[45]

On May 5, 1942, VH-CBA was reported to be the one of nine airplanes in service with the Air Transport Command. And on May 22nd, DAT made its first operational flight to New Guinea, where the Allies were in a desperate battle to halt the southward advance of Japanese ground forces attempting to occupy the island and cut the US military supply line to Australia.[46]

During this period, VH-CBA was used to fly troops and equipment from mainland Australia to Port Moresby, as well as for hauling supplies arriving at ports in south Australia, to the frontline battle zone locations where they were desperately needed.[47]

The advancing Japanese forces were within 32-miles of Port Moresby by September 18, 1942. Every available transport plane in Australia was pressed into service to airlift the Australian "Diggers" and their equipment from Brisbane to Port Moresby. Included were civil aircraft, as well as every operational bomber not required for tactical missions. Troops, equipment and supplies were airlifted daily to the forward areas in Papua New Guinea. Evacuation of casualties was carried out on the return flights, despite attacks by enemy aircraft.[48]

By November 1942, increasing numbers of DAT airplanes were now flying missions over the Owen Stanley Mountains in New Guinea, in support of the Allied offensive against the now retreating enemy forces. On December 12, 1942, the converted Flying Fortress VH-CBA was cited as the first four-engine aircraft to land troops and equipment at Buna.[49]

Courtesy Herbert S. Brownstein collection

B17C as Troop Transport

10

46th Troop Carrier Squadron

On January 14, 1943, members of 46th Troop Carrier Squadron of the US Fifth Air Force arrived in Townsville, with 56 new Douglas C-47s they had just flown across the Pacific. The planes were placed under the operational control of the Australian DAT and assigned to a new 317th Troop Carrier Group. Airplane B17C (VH-CBA), along with five old C-39s and a converted B-24 [Liberator bomber] were transferred to the 46th Troop Carrier Squadron of the 54th Troop Carrier Wing.[50]

In early February 1943, Captain Harold G. Slingsby and his crew, Lt. Vern Gidcumb, copilot, Lt. Jack Ogren, navigator, and crew chief S/Sgt.Frank Whelchel, flew the converted B-17C bomber (VH-CBA) from Port Moresby, PNG, to Townsville, Queensland. It was then turned over to the 46th Troop Carrier Squadron. Since Captain Slingsby's name appears frequently in subsequent reports about the veteran B-17C, it is likely he was its pilot from the first day the airplane was restored to non-combat transport duty.[51]

According to former flight mechanic, Del Sparrowe:

> Shortly after my arrival in Townsville, I was assigned as flight mechanic to the crew of B-17C (VH-CBA) — "Miss E.M.F." (every morning fix-it) so named, because almost eight-hours was spent on maintenance for every eight-hours of flying time.
>
> For about a month, we flew between Townsville and Port Moresby every day. Then in March, we were stationed in Mackay. Because there were no lodging facilities for us at the airfield, we had to live in town at one of the hotels.
>
> The flight from Townsville to Mackay was one of my most memorable. The pilot, Captain Slingsby, flew at no more than

1500 feet while I sat in glass nose section in the bombardiers seat. Being so far forward, the engines seemed quiet. And from the view in that position, it seemed like the world was rolling in front of me. It was like some 3-D video games we see today.

Capt. Slingsby was an airline pilot who flew in the Far East before the war. He came into the 46th TCS in February 1943 with B-17C (VH-CBA) and was its chief pilot until the first of June 1943, when he rotated back to the United States.

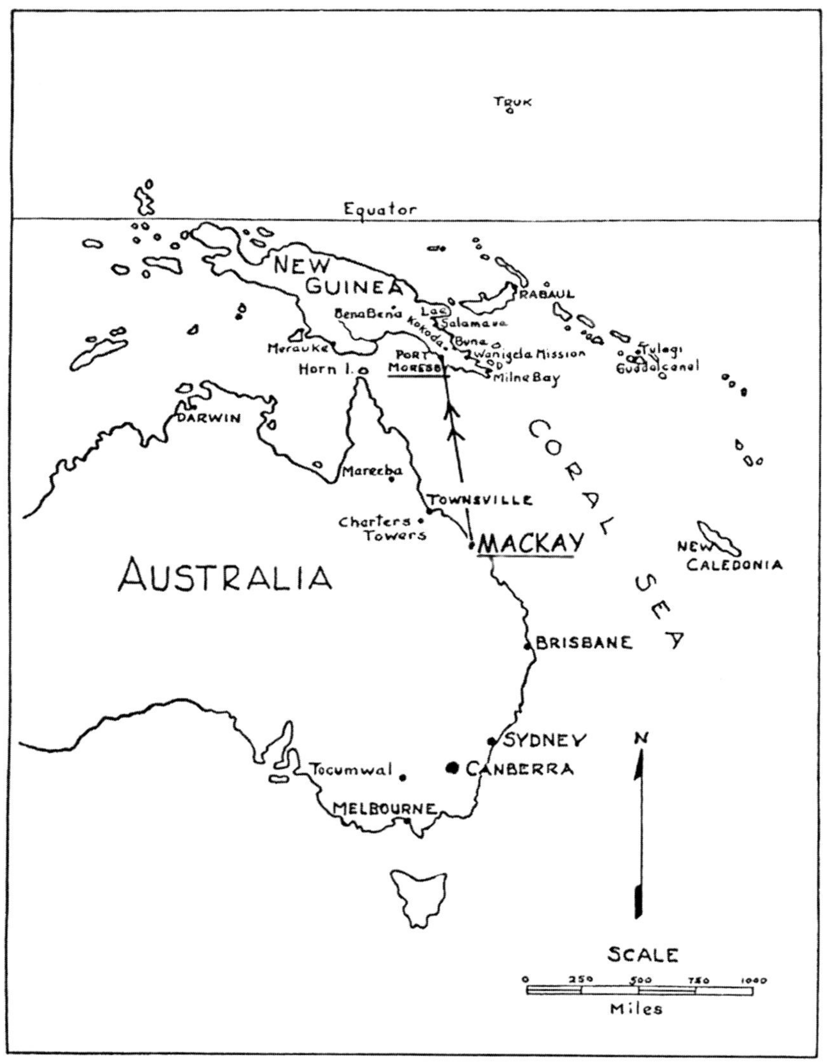

Map of Australia and New Guinea

> When we first got the plane, I flew down to Melbourne with it for some major maintenance. About all they did to the plane was paint it. You know the saying, "If you can't fix it, PAINT IT."
>
> On our return to Townsville, we stayed over-night in Sidney. That night, Captain Slingsby observed a freighter sailing under the Sidney Harbour Bridge. The next day, after we took-off, he said, "If a freighter could go under the bridge, so can I."
>
> He flew VH-CBA under the bridge. As we approached the bridge, sitting in the seat behind the pilot, the space beneath the bridge appeared to get smaller. But, as the Captain said, "If a freighter can do it, so can we." And we did!

Capt. Slingsby, S/Sgt. Whelchel, S/Sgt. Curtis, and B-17C remained with the 46th TCS, on temporary duty, to train others in the operation of this rare old bird. S/Sgt. Romeo 'Connie' Costantine and S/Sgt. Dale Curtis were assigned as new crew chiefs to VH-CBA. The plane and its crew flew their first cargo mission on February 5, 1943, when the airplane flew seven hours and thirty-five minutes to Port Moresby (MPL) and returned to Townsville (TVL).[52]

From mid-February to mid-March 1943, the aircraft added to its mounting total of flying hours when her crew began a series of 900-mile daily round trips over the Coral Sea, between Port Moresby and Townsville. Later in autumn, on March 12, 1943, VH-CBA was placed into service carrying troops between Mackay and Port Moresby, as part of the American Red Cross R&R (rest and recreation) program for the American troops stationed within the battle zone in New Guinea. The airplane flew almost every day on the 8½-hour round trip journey between the two destinations.[53]

The toll of flying hours began to mount on the aging aircraft. For the month of May 1943, in spite of being out of commission more than half of the time, VH-CBA flew some 9,744 miles in 75 1/2 hours, carrying 348 passengers. It was taken out of service at Mackay, on May 12, 1943, for a new fuel tank and some needed engine repairs.[54]

Over the next three weeks, the airplane underwent major maintenance at the Mackay civilian airport. A detachment of mechanics from the 46th Troop Carrier Squadron at Townsville, and their supervising Engineering officer, performed the work. The repairs included: replacement of the two inboard engines (Curtis-Wright, R-1820, Cyclone Radial engines) and one of the six, wing installed, fuel tanks. Three test flight then were performed; the first two involved rebuilt engines that failed.[55]

After a final flight test on June 13, 1943, using a new engine shipped from the States, aircraft B-17C (VH-CBA) was returned to flight duty.

The hour of the final catastrophe was at hand.

Endnotes

1. The Allied forces in the Southwest Pacific included Australian, Dutch, and American military units.

2. Martin Cadin, *Flying Forts*, New York: Balantine Books, 1968, 83.

3. *Ibid*, 83

4. U.S. Air Corps Inventory Card, RB-17C40-2072. Authority: SA-42-682 (dated: 10-1-41)

5. B-17C (40-2072) was one of the first 38 B-17C airplanes built by The Boeing Company in 1940. The first twenty Flying Fortresses were sent to England. Under terms of the US Lend-Lease Act of 1940, it became possible for the British to buy much needed war materials from the United States in their lonely stand against the seemingly invincible German forces. [Edward Jablonski, *Flying Fortress*, 26.]

6. Martin Cadin, *Flying Forts*, 144

7. Martin Cadin, *Flying Forts*, 167

8. Special Orders #1, 19th Bomb Group, Oct. 17, 1941

9. Martin Cadin, *Flying Forts*, 168

10. Walter D. Edmonds, *They Fought With What They Had*, 12.

11. Michael John Claringbould, *The Forgotten Fifth*, 105.

12. Christopher Shores and Brian Cull with Yasuho Izawa, *Bloody Shambles*, 63.

13. *Ibid*, 165.

14. "Summary of Air Actions in the Philippines and Netherlands East Indies," Army Air Force Historical Studies No. 29A, prepared by Asst. Chief of Air Staff Intelligence, Historical Division.

15. Martin Cadin, *Flying Forts*, 194]

16. Christopher Shores, *Bloody Shambles*, 177.

17. Army Air Forces Historical Studies No. 29A, Fifth Air Force, General Orders #20, 30 September 1942.

18. William L. White, *Queens Die Proudly*, 47.

19. Leon J. Long, letter to H. Brownstein, Sept. 23, 1995.

20. *Ibid,* Sept 23, 1995

21. History of the 19th Bomb Group, 1378

22. History Of 30th Bombardment Squadron, 19th Bombardment Group, December 1 to December 31, 1942.

23. Clark Field was completely evacuated by U.S. forces on December 24, 1941, although it was not until December 30th before the Japanese ground forces arrived. (H. Brownstein, *The Swoose*, 47).

24. Philip McKee, "*Warriors With Wings*", 31; Walter L. Edmonds, "*They Fought With What They Had*", 185; Army Air Force Historical Study No. 29A,"Summary of Air Actions", History of 19th Bombardment Group, 11.

25. Raymond G. Taborek, letter to Brownstein, June 30, 1995.

26. 19th Bombardment Group, Status Report, 11. Office of the CG, Ft. Washington, 19 October 1943, and 19th Bomb Group Diary,(Dec. 8, 1941 to Feb. 24, 1942).

27. "Flying Fortress of the 19th Bombardment Group," AAHS, Winter (1984).

28. Each engine had a dedicated fuel tank located in the wing. A feeder tank in each wing was used to replenish the engine fuel tanks in flight. The main spar is a metal beam that runs the length of each wing and provides it with much of its structural strength.

29. Walter D. Edmonds, *They Fought With What They Had*, 192.

30. Philip McKee, *Warrior With Wings*, 38.

31. *Ibid*, 39.

32. Capt. Alvin "Red" Mueller Collection, Sophienburg Museum and Archives, New Braunfelds, Texas.

33. Christopher Shores, *Bloody Shambles*, 196.

34. 19th Bombardment Group documents, 13 January 1942.

35. Pat Robinson, *The Fight For New Guinea*, 35.

36. "RSL Uncovers Details of Wartime Plane," *The Daily Mercury*, Dec. 15, 1993.

37. *The Economist*, June 17, 1995.

38. History of Air Transport, Allied Air Forces Southwest Pacific, and, Squadron History of 21st Troop Carrier Squadron, 322nd Troop Carrier Wing, 24 May 1945.

39. Walter D. Edmonds, *They Fought With What They Had*, 256.

40. Major General Lewis H. Brereton, commander of the US Army Far East Air Force (FEAF) from October 1941 to February 23, 1942, was responsible for all US Army Air Forces activities in the Southwest Pacific. [Roger G. Miller, "A Pretty Damn Able Commander, Lewis Hyde Brereton – Part II," *Air Power History*, Vol. 48, No. 1, Spring 2001, 27-35.]

41. Lewis H. Brereton, *The Brereton Diaries: The War in the Air in the Pacific,* New York: William Morrow and Company, 1946, 76-77.

42. John H. Mitchell, "Flying Fortresses of 19th Bomb Group," American Aviation Historical Society, Winter 1984.

43. John Lardner, "Lardner Goes To The War": The Japs Don't like the Sting of the Fortress, *Newsweek*, April 6, 1942.

44. 317th Troop Carrier Group Operations Report, May 1943, and discussions with Dana Bell, National Air & Space Museum, 1993.

45. Geoffrey Perret, *Winged Victory: The Army Air Forces in World War II*, New York: Random House, 1993, 162.

46. John H. Mitchell, "Flying Fortresses of the 19th"; and James D. Rorrison, *They Fought With What They Had*', 256.

47. History of 374th Troop Carrier Group (S10284); Historical Record of Air Transport Command, 2 July 1942; and Air Transport Command Operations Order, No. 21, 21 May 1942.

48. Air Transport Command Operations Order, No. 21, 21 May 1942.

49. 374th Troop Carrier Group Citation, January 7, 1943.

50. History of Directorate For Air Transport, Allied Air Forces in Southwest Pacific Area, 322nd Troop Carrier Wing, WG-322-HI; Unit History, Roll A0978, (Sq-TR-CARR-46-HI).

51. Del Sparrowe, email to Bruce Litte and R. Cutler, April 16, 2003.

52. Romeo Costantine and Delmer Sparrow, interview with R. Cutler, 46th TCS Reunion, Louisville, KY, Sept. 30, 2000.

53. Romeo Costantine and Delmer Sparrow, interview with R. Cutler, 46th TCS Reunion, Louisville, KY, Sept. 30, 2000.

54. History of the 374th Troop Carrier Group, 46th Troop Carrier Squadron, Army Air Forces, Report of Operations, 1-31 May 1943, Appendix C; Roll 1223;

55. Paul Maynard, email message to R. Cutler, Nov. 16, 2000.

PART 2

The Air Crash

Courtesy Sam Cutler collection

Queen Street, City of Mackay in 1943

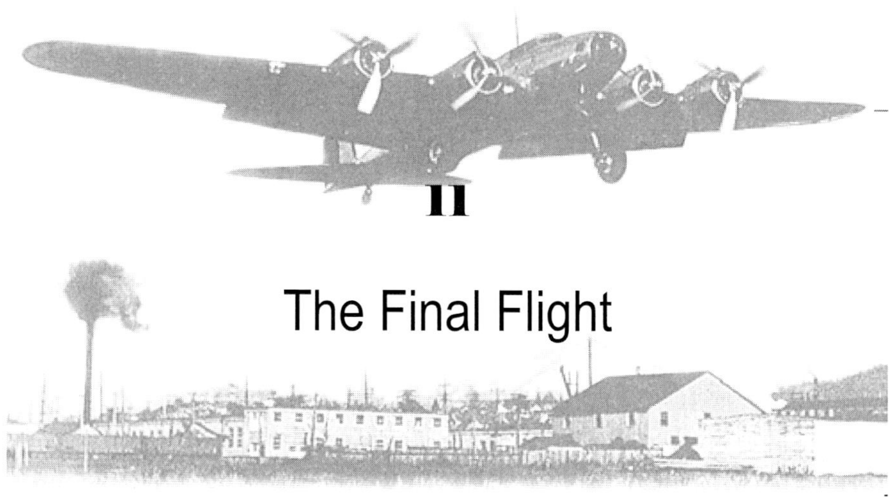

11

The Final Flight

Early in the morning of June 14, 1943, before the first light of dawn, six crewmen and thirty-five passengers boarded the old, war-torn airplane now known as VH-CBA. It was operated by a detachment of airmen from the 46th Troop Carrier Squadron, based in Townsville, and had been grounded for nearly a month for major maintenance. During the previous week, the plane was thoroughly inspected and a test flight had been made the previous day. The aircraft checked out to the satisfaction of the pilots, the engineering officer, and the crew chief.[1]

One by one, each of the four engines of the former Flying Fortress bomber began to start. At a signal from 1/Lt. Vern J. Gidcumb, the pilot, the wheel chocks were removed, the brakes released, and the heavy airplane began to lumber forward over the rough turf as it taxied to the threshold of Runway 23, (4700-ft. long), which rolled in a southwest direction.

The weather was misty, ceiling 250 feet, with light winds and some patches of ground fog reported in the area. Aligning its nose to the west, the pilot checked the controls and applied the brakes. And in accordance with standard operating procedures, the flight crew ran each engine up to its full takeoff power while checking magnetos.

Satisfied that all systems were operating normally, the copilot Flight Officer William C. Erb released the lever that locked the tail-wheel to stop it from swiveling during the take-off roll.

The last two passengers to enter the plane were Cpl. Marlin D. Metzger and Cpl. Foye K. Roberts. Flying was not new to them; it was part of their jobs as engine mechanics with the 6th Troop Carrier Squadron. (The unit had been among the first to arrive in New Guinea, six month earlier, when the Japanese had advanced to the Kokoda Pass only 30 miles from Port Moresby).

After climbing aboard the two went forward, squatting next to the rear radio compartment bulkhead so the tail would not be too heavy. Corporal Roberts spread his legs apart and his buddy Metzger sat "toboggan style" between them. Being a former Bible schoolteacher he bowed his head, as it was natural for him to give a silent prayer each time he was in a plane at takeoff.[2]

The pilot pushed the four throttles forward to their stops. The large dark airplane pointed its sharp nose to the southwest, and with a great surge of power, soared into the air. There was so much noise the crowded passengers could neither talk nor understand each other. When airborne, the pilot uncovered the landing-gear toggle switch to activate the electric motors that pull the wheels up to a retracted position. However, on this occasion, it is not clear whether the landing-gear was retracted, since the airplane climbed only a few hundred feet, leveled off, and then it made two level 90-degree left turns.

B-17C Taking Off

Observers on the ground watched as the big, olive drab painted B-17C airplane began to bank, turn to the south, and then take up a heading that would carry it back over the airport and on to its northerly route over the Coral Sea toward Port Moresby, New Guinea.

Then, something went wrong. In horror, those on the ground watched as the huge airplane suddenly nosed over and flew into the ground.

"This is my version of what happened the morning of 14th June 1943." — Percey Webb, local Mackay resident. He said that he was delivering meat for his employer by bicycle near the airport.

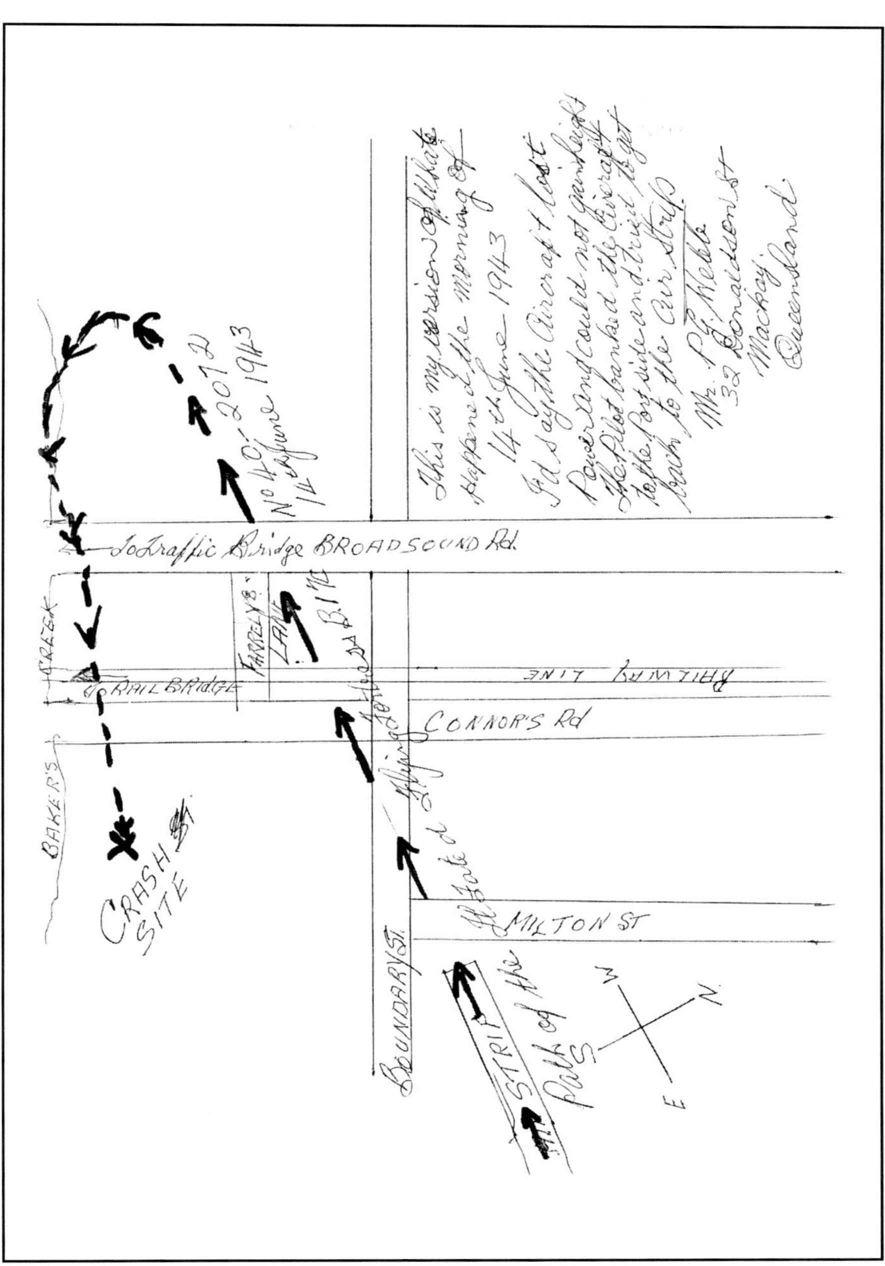

"This is my version of what happened the morning of June 14 1943"
— Percy Webb, Mackay resident - June 4 2002

There were other witnesses apart from Percy Webb. A woman rounding up her cows for morning milking on the family farm was another eyewitness to the crash. Years later, she told a local newspaper reporter:

> One could set your clock by the arrival and departure of the B-17's. From four o'clock in the afternoon they would appear from the north and, from five o'clock in the morning, the roar of their engines could be heard as they prepared for the flight northwards.
>
> She went on to say, "normally the Fortresses gained altitude quickly, their noses pointing upwards." But on this morning, after the aircraft had risen to about 300 feet, she realized that it was in trouble. As it made a sweep to the west and north after takeoff, she sensed that the pilot could not lift the nose.
>
> Sitting in the saddle, unable to do anything but watch, Miss Rogers followed the flight of the Fortress in the fateful minutes before it fell from the sky, crashing on to what is now the site of the Thomas Borthwick and Sons abattoir (meat processing plant).
>
> She could picture the pilot ("poor devil," she called him) desperately battling with the controls to gain altitude. The engines then began backfiring and finally the last backfire illuminated the entire fuselage from cockpit to tail and the fortress fell almost horizontally from the sky. It disappeared from view and there was a tremendous crash. Miss Rogers said that in a straight line she was about a mile and half from the crash site but she could feel the ground reverberating under herself and the horse. She said, "the whole countryside was lit up by a brilliant flash of fire." [3]

One man said he happened to be following the flight and that the plane wasn't gaining height and turned in a southerly direction.[4] Another person, Mr. Pat Carrol, saw the plane from a different location.

> I had been riding my bicycle on Nebo Road to Wally Rix's property, at Chelona, when I heard the plane take off from the airport. I saw it moving, but it seemed a bit slow in getting up in the air. Then it almost came to a stop when it started to fall. It crashed into the trees and into the old Bakers Creek bridge. One bloke survived, and the others were all killed.[5]

Of the 41 men aboard, only one survived. The flaming impact area was found in a scrubby tree-lined paddock near a bridge just outside the town of Bakers Creek, five miles south of Mackay.

According to two official US Fifth Air Force reports:

1. "The ship was performing in a satisfactory manner when, for some reason, it dove into the ground and exploded." [6]

2. "Taking off from Mackay, Queensland, on a routine flight, the B-17C, CBA, crashed killing 40 of her 41 passengers.

This catastrophe was the worst ever suffered in the S.W.P.A. (Southwest Pacific Area)." [7]

Courtesy Al Soxman

B-17C Flying Fortress (VH-CBA) crash site at Bakers Creek on June 14 1943

Official Statements

The first call to local police came at 6:05 a.m. from Joan Harris, the young daughter of the proprietor of the Harris Store at Bakers Creek, to the effect that an airplane had just crashed into the nearby Harris Paddock and appeared to be on fire. Hearing the noise and seeing a rising column of smoke, her father, Gordon Harris, told her to call the police.

A local sugarcane farm worker, Arnold Radcliffe Bragg, was one of the first people to arrive at the crash site. He found a survivor, Corporal Foye K. Roberts, lying face down on the ground. He rolled the soldier onto his back and told him to lie still. Later, while tending to another still-living crash victim, Bragg noticed that Cpl. Roberts had gotten to his feet and was walking about in a daze, but relatively unhurt.[8]

In the wreckage of the B-17C VH-CBA, a military policeman recovered a manufacturer's data plate identifying the ill-fated airplane as: "United States Army Air Corps B-17C, Serial Number 40-2072, thus positively identifying the wreck.[9]

Courtesy of Lawrence Keating Collection

GI's at the crash site

All told, the crash was considered at the time (mid-1943) to be "the biggest air crash in American Air Transport History to date." [10] This forgotten WW II mishap, according to the *Air Force Times,* "earned several grim distinctions: In terms of loss of life, it was the worst crash ever involving a U.S. bomber, the worst aircraft loss in the Southwest Pacific war, and nearly sixty years later, the worst aviation disaster in Australia's history." [11]

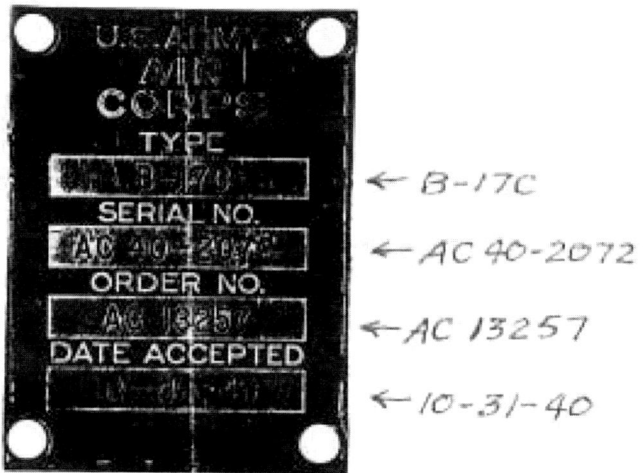

Boeing Aircraft Company's indentificatin tag for B-17C (40-2072) found at Bakers Creek Crash site on June 14, 1943

News of the tragic event was withheld from the American public by wartime censorship. Although it was common knowledge throughout the Mackay district, there was no mention of the disaster in either the Australian or the American press or radio. However, on the day after the crash, the local Mackay newspaper, remarkable for its discretion, stated simply in a brief Ambulance Notice that "an American serviceman had been injured during his visit to Mackay" -- a reference to Corporal Foye K. Roberts, the only survivor of the crash. Together with a brief editorial, "We Share Their Grief," [12] these two news items were the only public reference to the B-17C aviation disaster published during the war.[13]

An Ironic Note

S/Sgt. Romeo "Connie" Costantine, a crew chief with the detachment of 46th Troop Carrier Squadron personnel stationed at Mackay, was told the evening before the fateful flight that VH-CBA's former crew chief, S/Sgt. Frank E. Whelchel, would replace him on the next day's flight to Port Moresby. Costantine said "S/Sgt Whelchel needed the flight time to qualify for his monthly flight pay; he was scheduled to return to the U.S. later in June and probably would not find another flight assignment before then." [14]

On the morning of June 14th, about 9:00 a.m., S/Sgt. Costantine was having breakfast at the American Red Cross Centre in Mackay when he and his companions were informed that his airplane, B-17C (VH-CBA), had just crashed. Later that day, he departed as ordered by plane for Townsville on a new assignment, realizing that "Whelchel's fate had granted him life." [15]

Courtesy Al Soxman

Bakers Creek Crash Pile of Junk

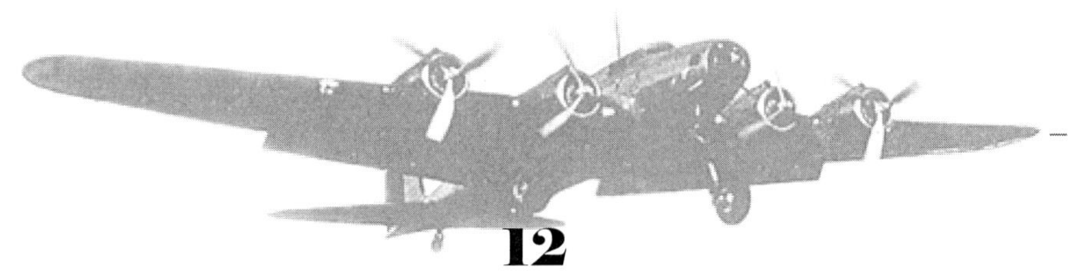

12

Assessment of the Calamity

The crash stunned the people in Mackay, particularly the military. There were few eyewitnesses to the calamity and much confusion. Captain Samuel Cutler, the executive officer of the US Army Rest Area at Mackay, recorded some details of the incident in his personal wartime dairy.[16]

The day before the crash, he wrote:

> Sunday, June 13th, 1943
>
> Saw CBA Flying Fortress test hopping over us. Our Major Diller was aboard with Lt. Gidcumb as pilot. The B-17 was in good shape after having been laid up for almost a month while getting a special gas tank from the U.S. The plane was known as *Miss EMF* of "every morning fix-it" fame.
>
> Out gardening in the afternoon. My garden looks swell. Corn plants up ten inches in three weeks almost. Early to bed fora 4 AM wake-up call as OD tomorrow. Oh hum!

Then, the following day:

> Monday, ** JUNE 14th **, 1943
>
> What a day and a TRAGIC one. Up at 4 AM and lined up 35 enlisted and two officers to go on CBA to Moresby for 6:00 AM take-off from Mackay Aerodrome. The weather was misty and one of those things DID HAPPEN. Yes, at 6:02 AM, two minutes after I turned my back on the CBA plane (same one I saw yesterday) it crashed into some woods five miles away and exploded killing 40 people, with only one saved. Biggest air crash in American air transport history, to date.

> Pilot error and poor visibility. As OD, I put the men on the ship and so had a direct part in sealing their fate. Also I was at the scene of the crash and saw the mangled bodies, killed while flying at 200 mile per hour. Terrible.

Army personnel conducted cleanup activities for the next few days. They worked under high pressure, collecting bodies, personal effects, interviewing witnesses — and keeping quiet about the details of the crash.[17]

Capt. Cutler's diary notes continue:

> June 15th (Tuesday)
>
> All kinds of telephone calls from Brisbane and Townsville. Arrival of planes to carry 40 dead bodies to Townsville (205 miles away). Scenes at the Morgue identifying bodies, etc. Very gruesome, especially as to mangled bodies. Found a book at the crash scene titled *The General Died at Dawn*. Very significant (!)
>
> Everything hush-hush. Largest single number of dead so far, in one airplane. The one survivor is recuperating. Lucky, lucky fellow.
>
> June 16th (Wednesday)
>
> Visited scene of the airplane crash at Bakers Creek, 5-miles away, with Major Diller and Lt. Neighbors, Aerodrome Engineering Officer. Based on our observations, it seemed as though the crash occurred through poor visibility and error in pilot's judgment of altitude, while banking to make turn. Saw where the left wing sheared through the treetops, lost part of the wing, lost one engine then two more engines, then burst into flames and exploded when gas tanks caught fire. Also examined wreckage for clues. Found some gruesome token, the lower left leg of a body with stocking and shoe. Also took pictures of scenes for official investigation. Very gruesome tokens all strewn about. Blackened trees, blood spots, personal effects, etc. Very very tragic. Greatest single disaster in airplanes in history of aviation.
>
> June 17th (Thursday)
>
> Telephones ringing all day from official sources to check up on all details of crash. Bodies had been sent via airplane to TVL [Townsville] for burial. Reports of Death Certificates had to be made out. All sorts of details, especially inquiries as to next of kin, etc.
>
> Censored ten letters of victims showing normal hopes and desires. Too bad! One boy has a sister living on High Street in my

home town [Springfield, Mass.] "Tileston"- 147 High Street. Will look her up some day. [18]

All news suppressed in this vicinity. Papers and radio station clamped down. Life goes on just the same.

As a result of this episode, I decided then and there to buy me $5,000 more insurance. Innocent people do get killed in wartime, even while traveling by air. Safety First - for my family, if not for me. I've seen enough to prove its value in war.

On the next day, Capt. Cutler reports in his diary a visit to the Mackay District Hospital with Major John Diller, the Detachment commander, Major Siegel, the surgeon, and Lt. Eugene Neighbors, airport engineering officer. They went to interview the lone crash survivor -- Corporal Foye K. Roberts.[19]

June 18th (Friday)

Had a rare experience today. Went over to the Mackay District Hospital with Major Siegel (the surgeon), Major Diller and Lt. Neighbors (four of us) to interview the lone and lucky survivor of the airplane crash. his name is Corporal Foye Roberts.

Loa and behold, as we got to his bed we saw his dog tags and a lucky four-leaf clover token dangling over his head. He sure was lucky. Flying in a fog at 200 miles per hour, striking the treetops and having the Flying Fortress explode and he the only survivor of 41 passengers. He was very rational and spoke intelligently.

Not dazed at all, just normal.

He knew me as the OD who put him on the plane. Knew all the problems. We agreed that his seat in the radio section of the plane "boxed" him in safely against everything when it crashed.

June 19th - 25th

Well, the crash is now being slowly forgotten. All the reports are in. Now back to routine again, but not for long.

We received a visit from the Base Inspector, to be with us a week. He certainly knew his job but got in our hair by checking on all details minutely. Spoiled our plans for a kangaroo hunting trip for the weekend. Made us pull an inspection of both men and vehicles. Major Diller and I both busy but had to cater to him. Part of the Army policy; visiting firemen.

Managed to work in my Victory Garden in spare moments. Coming along fine. Edna keeps it watered. Her father let a horse come in "to mow the grass" and he stepped over a part of it.

> Horses, cows, cats and dogs have free run of most Australia.
>
> Darn them!

Stemming from his agricultural roots during the Great Depression in the United States during the 1930s, Capt. Cutler kept a small vegetable garden at the home of John Johnson, a local host family in Mackay. During his separation from home and to relieve the stress of wartime life, he worked in his borrowed "Victory Garden" in spare moments.

Finally, barely two weeks after the tragic incident, Capt. Cutler wrote: [20]

> June 26th - July 1st
>
> No one speaks about the air crash. All forgotten, officially. All reports in and life goes on just the same.
>
> Picked up a souvenir from the crash; the siren horn that tells when the wheels are down ready for a landing. Also found a souvenir that illustrates the force of the crash; a playing card that was hurled out of a pack of cards and landed in the fibers of a splintered tree and forced halfway through. Best to forget some of the other things.

The Aftermath

For those in Mackay who saw the twisted wreckage and smoking brush fires at the scene, the cause of the crash remained a mystery. No official US Army investigation report of the incident has yet been found. Because of wartime security, news of the crash was not reported in the United States. During World War II, when no other cause could be acknowledged, "pilot error" was frequently cited, by default.[21]

Years later, a local Mackay newspaper reported that because it [the Flying Fortress] was military rather than a civil air crash prevented investigation by the Australian aviation authorities.[22]

Following the end of World War II, and for many years thereafter, the "Flying Fortress air crash" became more a part of Mackay's folklore, handed down from generation to generation, than a publicly known and reported event. In the early 1990s, the crash became more widely known through the efforts of the Bakers Creek Memorial Committee.[23] They decided to build a memorial to the forty lost American servicemen at Bakers Creek, to coincide with local observances of North Queensland's 50th Anniversary Commemoration of the WW II Battle of the Coral Sea, in May 1992.[24]

In the course of their work, the members of the Committee uncovered information about the crash and several possible causes, which are presented below and discussed in chapter 13.

Mackay Police Investigation

A significant report [25] was uncovered in 1993. It is the only official document containing eyewitness testimony and was prepared by the Mackay police department shortly after the crash. The report was promptly sent through official US Army channels to the Commanding General of the Fifth Air Force.[26]

The report is based upon the testimony of several witnesses, the observations of police personnel investigating the crash site, and information provided by the USAAF engineering officer assigned to supervise the military flight operations at the Mackay airport.

The primary purpose of the Mackay Police report, it appears, was to ascertain whether sabotage was involved. The conclusion: "No suspicion or possibility of sabotage; the whole occurrence being entirely accidental." [27]

Removal of the Dead

Caskets draped with the American flag were buried in the Belgian Gardens Cemetery, in Townsville, 400 miles north, soon after the crash. They were later disinterred in mid-1945, before the Pacific war ended, and reburied in the American Cemetery at Ipswich, near Brisbane. In late 1947, these human remains were again disinterred, placed in metal caskets, and then transported aboard U.S. Army transports to American soil. Thirteen of the forty Bakers Creek crash victims were off-loaded at Honolulu, Territory of Hawaii, and

Caskets draped with American flags are carried to temporary graveside at Belgian Gardens Cemetery in Townsville following the crash of the Flying Fortress (VH-VBA) at Mackay on June 14 1943

laid to final rest in the National Memorial Cemetery of the Pacific. The remaining caskets were taken to Fort Mason, San Francisco, then shipped via rail to various Army General Depots for final shipment to local funeral homes previously selected by each serviceman's "next-of-kin." [28]

The families of the forty dead servicemen were notified that they could arrange to have their loved ones' bodies buried in cemeteries near their homes. 27 of the 40 casualties were later reburied in local cemeteries in the continental United States.

Courtesy Teddy W. Hanks and Colin E. Benson

State	Name	Final Resting Place
ARKANSAS	Sgt. Carl A. Cunningham	National Memorial Cemetery of the Pacific, HI
CALIFORNIA	T/5 George A. Ehrmann	Golden Gate National Cemetery, San Bruno, CA
	F/0 William C. Erb	Pomona Cemetery, Pomona, CA
CONNECTICUT	* Sgt. David E. Tileston	National Memorial Cemetery of the Pacific, HI
COLORADO	* Sgt. Dean H. Buss	Hillside Cemetery, Julesburg, COL
FLORIDA	Pfc. Jerome Abraham	Riverside Memorial Cemetery, Jacksonville, FL
GEORGIA	S/Sgt. Frank E. Whelchel	Lyons City Cemetery, Lyons, GA
ILLINOIS	* S/Sgt. Lovell D. Curtis	National Memorial Cemetery of the Pacific, HI
	* 1/Lt Vern J. Gidcumb	Wolf Creek Cemetery, Eldorado, IL
	Pfc. Norman J. Goetz	St. Mary's Cemetery, Chicago, IL
KENTUCKY	T/Sgt. James A. Copeland	National Memorial Cemetery of the Pacific, HI
	* Sgt. Leo E. Fletcher	Crayne Cemetery, Crayne, KY
	Pvt. Raymond D. Longabaugh	National Memorial Cemetery of the Pacific, HI
MICHIGAN	Pfc. Frederick C. Sweet	White Chapel Cemetery, Oakland County, MI
MISSOURI	Pfc. Kenneth W. Mann	Jefferson National Cemetery, Jefferson City, MO
	* Pfc. Charles M. Williams	IOOF Cemetery, Charleston, MO
NEBRASKA	* Cpl. Marlin D. Metzger	Hillcrest Cemetery, Omaha, NE
NEW JERSEY	Pfc. Vernon Johnson	National Memorial Cemetery of the Pacific, HI
NEW YORK	* Capt. John 0. Berthold	Woodlawn National Cemetery, Elmira, NY
	Cpl. Charles W. Sampson	Calvary Cemetery, Port Leyden, NY
NORTH CAROLINA	Cpl. Franklin F. Smith	National Memorial Cemetery of the Pacific, HI
NORTH DAKOTA	Maj. George N. Powell	Arlington National Cemetery, Ft. Myer, VA
	* Pfc. Arnold Seidel	Ft. Snelling National Cemetery, Minneapolis, MN
OHIO	2/Lt. Jack A. Ogren	cemetery unknown
OKLAHOMA	* Cpl. Jacob 0. Skaggs, Jr.	Rose Hill Cemetery, Tulsa, OK
PENNSYLVANIA	* Pvt. James E. Finney	Laurel Hill Cemetery, Erie, PA
	* T/Sgt. Alfred H. Frezza	Calvary Cemetery, Altoona, PA
	* Sgt. Donald B. Kyper	Riverside Cemetery, Huntingdon, PA
	Pfc. Frank S. Penksa	National Cemetery of the Pacific, HI
	Sgt. Anthony Rudnick	Beverly National Cemetery, Beverly, NJ
	Cpl. Raymond H. Smith	National Memorial Cemetery of the Pacific, HI
SOUTH CAROLINA	T/5 William A. Briggs	National Memorial Cemetery of the Pacific, HI
	Pfc. John W. Parker	Greenlawn Memorial Park, Columbia, SC
TENNESSEE	* Pvt. Charles D. Montgomery	National Memorial Cemetery of the Pacific, HI
TEXAS	S/Sgt. Charlie 0. LaRue	National Memorial Cemetery of the Pacific, HI
	* Ruben L. Vaughn	Rabon Chapel Cemetery, Montgomery, TX
	* *Cpl. Foye K. Roberts*	*Sole Survivor, Wichita Falls, TX*
WASHINGTON	* S/Sgt. Roy A. Hatlen	National Memorial Cemetery of the Pacific, HI
WEST VIRGINIA	* S/Sgt. John W. Hilsheimer	Arlington National Cemetery, VA
	Cpl. Edward Tenny	Big Bend Cemetery, Upshur County, WV
	* Pfc. Dale Van Fosson	Grafton National Cemetery, Grafton, WV

Casualty list and burial sites

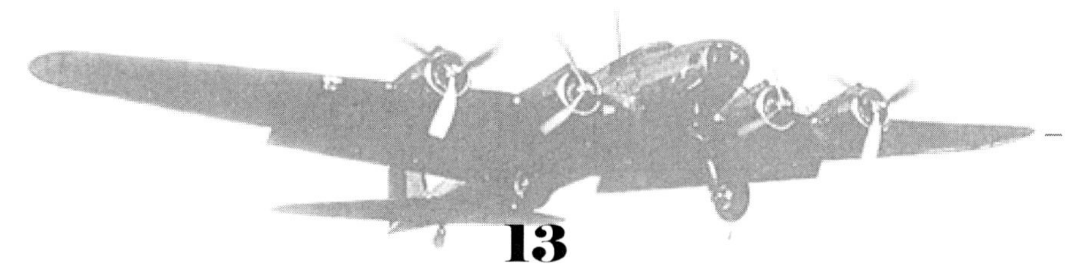

13

Probable Causes of Crash

The Mackay Police report, however, fails to mention any technical evaluation of the wreckage from which the cause of the crash could be determined. Indeed, more facts were needed to substantiate and to permit analysis of the anecdotal information obtained. Little information was publicly released, no record of the US Army's investigation has been found, and there is scant mention of the crash in the histories of the 317th Troop Carrier Group and the 46th Troop Carrier Squadron.

It is therefore difficult to reconstruct events surrounding a plane crash that happened sixty years ago in the middle of World War II in Australia. At the time of the crash, VH-CBA (40-2072) was the only B-17C Flying Fortress still flying in the Southwest Pacific. To interview pilots who flew this early model of the B-17 airplane is no longer possible. The subsequent Flying Fortress E through H models had unique flight characteristics that were significantly different from the earlier and smaller C model. We may never know the full story of what went wrong with VH-CBA on June 14, 1943.

However, several researchers [29] working in the United States and in Australia during the past decade have recently discovered several World War II-era documents, containing many useful facts. Microfilm copies of those now declassified secret records confirm: [30]

> 1) The loss of B-17C (VH-CBA) near Mackay, Queensland, Australia, on 14 June 1943;
>
> 2) The loss of its six-member crew, by name, from the 46th Troop Carrier Squadron, 517th Troop Carrier Group, Fifth Air Force.

They are:

1/Lt Vern J. Gidcumb, pilot
F/O William C. Erb, copilot
2/Lt Jack A. Ogren, navigator
S/Sgt Lovell D. Curtis, crew chief
S/Sgt Frank E. Whelchel, crew chief
Sgt. David E. Tileston, radio operator

3) That senior crew chief [S/Sgt. Frank E. Whelchel] on detached duty from the 22TCS, had been with the plane since early February 1942;

4) That there was only one survivor [Cpl. Foye K. Roberts];

5) That the airplane had a new gas tank and two new engines installed and checked-out during a test hop the day before the accident;

6) That the catastrophe was the worst ever suffered in the SWPA. [Southwest Pacific Area, during WW II].

In addition, we also were able to interview three former USAAF flying crew chiefs from the WW II 46th Troop Carrier Squadron. They are: Romeo "Connie" Costantine, Delmer L. Sparrowe, and Paul L. Maynard. They actually flew and did maintenance work on B-17C (VH-CBA) at Mackay in 1943.[31] The information they provided about the airplane (called *Miss EMF* – Every Morning Fix-It) provided several valuable facts and realistic opinions about the condition of the plane and its final flight.[32] (see their comments at end of chapter 13)

Analysis of Findings

Five scenarios describing the possible causes of the crash are presented and discussed below. They are drawn from the historic facts, published statements, and the related opinions that have thus far been received.

They are, not in order of probability:

Scenario A - Pitot-Tube Malfunction

Scenario B - Aircraft Weight/Balance Overload

Scenario C - Engine Fire Emergency

Scenario D - Engine Power Failure

Scenario E – Pilots' Proficiency

The basic question lingers: Why did the pilot of B-17C (VH-CBA), just after takeoff and while still flying at very low altitude, elect to make two 90-degree turning maneuvers that led to the crash?

Scenario A – Pitot Tube Malfunction

Each B-17 was equipped with devices called "pitot-tubes," installed at two places outside the airplane. Smaller aircraft of that era were equipped with Pitot tubes mounted on a single probe. The ambient air entering the tubes was used to activate three sets of airspeed indicators and altimeters. They were located on the pilot, copilot, and navigator instrument panels. When combined with the "static ports", they created the Pitot-Static System, which gave the crew its airspeed and altitude information.

To prevent foreign objects from entering the tubes, cloth sleeves usually covered them while the airplane was parked. Routinely, the cloth sleeves were removed from the two external tubes by the crew chief, or by a member of the ground crew during the preflight check of the airplane before the engines were started.

Failure to remove a pitot-tube sleeve would result in an inoperative airspeed indicator, a device critical to properly controlling the airplane. If this condition had occurred, the first warning to the pilot would be during the takeoff roll, when he or the copilot would notice the inoperative instruments and abort the takeoff.

If unable to safely continue the flight to Port Moresby without airspeed indicators, the pilot would then have had to initiate a return to the landing field. Since no technical evaluation of the wreckage was made (the cloth pitot-tube covers were destroyed in the crash fire) there is no evidence to assign weight to this scenario as a probable cause.

[One fellow researcher, H. Brownstein, actually experienced an event of this nature. Fortunately, it occurred during daylight hours and in clear weather].

Each B-17C had two pitot-static systems; one activated the navigator's panel instruments, the other activated the pilot's and copilot's flight indicators. The two pitot probes were contained in streamlined housings attached to masts extending away from the fuselage, below the bombardier's position, on the right and left sides of the aircraft's nose. Impact air entered the front port. Another port, at the rear of the streamlined housing, provided static air pressure. The static port also supplied the barometric pressure to the altimeter.

If just one protective cloth cover had not been removed, it is possible the accuracy of the pilot's altimeters also would have been adversely affected.

Scenario B - Aircraft Weight/Balance Overload

Aircraft control in flight is sensitive to the location of its center of gravity, called the "CG." The CG is the point along the centerline of the fuselage about which the total weight of the flying aircraft would balance, if simply

AIR TRANSPORT CONTROL

TOWNSVILLE

MANIFEST

Copy No 9

AIRCRAFT TYPE B-17-C CALL LETTERS MACKAY VHC BA DATE 14/6/43

ARRIVED FROM MAPLE TIME 0625/Z/13/5

DEPARTED FOR MAPLE TIME 2000/Z/13/5

PILOT 1st Lt. V.J. GIDCUMB WEIGHT EMPTY 30,400

CO-PILOT F/O W.C. ERB FUEL (1200) 7,200

ENGINEER S SGT FRANK WHELCHEL / S SGT L DALE CURTISS OIL (134) 1,005

RADIO OPR. SGT DAVE TILESTON CREW (6) 1,100

NAVIGATOR 2nd Lt. JACK A OGREN CREW BAGGAGE 100

TOTAL (BASIC WEIGHT) 39,805

AUTH.	DESCRIPTION	NUMBER	DEST.	WEIGHT	
(Added in Pencil)	CORP SMITH, FRANKLIN F.	14056644	MBY	200	405th Bom.Sq.38th Bomb Gp.
	CAPT BERTHOLD, JOHN O.	0-362697	MBY	200	8th Ftr. Sq.
	MAJOR POWELL, GEORGE N	0-188378	"	"	Hq 49th Ftr Gp.
	CORP RUDNICK, ANTHONY	33074860	"	"	Co. "A" 565th Sig. Bn.
	S SGT LA RUE, CHARLIE O	17031767	"	"	8th Ftr. Sq. 49th Ftr. Gp.
	SGT CUNNINGHAM, CARL A.	37099012	"	"	8th Ftr. Sq. 49th Ftr. Gp.
	PVT ABRAHAM, JEROME	34057460	"	"	Hq 49th Ftr. Group
	PVT JOHNSON, VERNON	32202796	"	"	Co. "A" 440th Sig. Bn.
	T SGT FREZZA, ALFRED H.	6949396	"	"	27th Dep. Rep. Sq.
	PVT FINNEY, JAMES E.	13041209	"	"	" " " "
	CORP SKAGGS, JACOB O	20831453	"	"	" " " "
	T/5 EHRMANN, GEORGE A.	39010163	"	"	Sig. Hq.Co.5th Ftr. Com.
	PVT MANN, KENNETH W.	17034812	"	"	374th Serv Sq.36th Serv Gp.
Crossed out pencil	~~PFC GILPATRICK, KARL F~~	~~13002268~~	~~"~~	~~"~~	(Crossed out in pendil)
	PFC WILLIAMS, CHARLES M.	37130251	"	"	455th Serv Sq.
	PFC SWEET, FREDERICK C.	36170582	"	"	46th Ord.Co. 481st Serv. Sq.
	PFC GOETZ, NORMAN J.	36314652	"	"	480th Serv. Sq.
	PVT MONTGOMERY, CHARLES D.	14070519	"	"	7th Ftr. Sq. 49th Ftr. Gp.
	PFC PARKER, JOHN W.	34096008	"	"	809th Chem Co.
	CORP TENNEY, EDWARD	15089172	"	"	479th Serv. Sq.
	PVT LONGABOUGH, RAYMOND	35492803	"	"	842nd Eng. Av. Bn.
	S SGT HATLEN, ROY A.	19074000	"	"	40th Ftr. Sq. 35th Ftr. Gp.
	CORP SMITH, RAYMOND H.	13010165	"	"	" " " " " "
	S SGT HILSHEIMER, JOHN W.	15065480	"	"	" " " " " "
	SGT BUSSE, DEAN	18069312	"	"	" " " " " "
	SGT FLETCHER, LEO E.	15081810	"	"	405th Bomb Sq. 38th Bomb Gp.
	PFC VANFOSSEN, DALE	35207505	"	"	1160th QM Co. 8th Serv. Gp.
	PFC SAMPSON, CHARLES W.	12044272	"	"	11th Serv Sq. 8th Serv. Gp.
	T SGT COPELAND, JAMES A.	15043898	"	"	Hq Sq 8th Serv Gp.
	PVT VAUGHN, RUBEN L.	38205068	"	"	Hq Sq 5th Ftr. Command
	PFC SIEDEL, ARNOLD	37163000	"	"	415th Signal Co. 5th A.F.
	T/5 BRIGGS, WILLIAM A.	34011307	"	"	1037th Sig. Co. 478th Serv Sq
	PFC PENKSA, FRANK S.	33172883	"	"	6th Tr. Car. Sq. 374th Tr.Car.
	CORP METZGER, MARLEN D.	17040608	"	"	" " " " " " "Gp.
(Only man alive)	CORP ROBERTS, FOYE K.	18065977	"	"	" " " " " " "
	SGT KYPER, DONALD B.	33080317	"	"	405th Bomb Sq. 38th Bomb Gp
	MKY BAG, MAIL	1	MBY	5	

TOTAL (PAYLOAD) 7,005

GROSS WEIGHT 46,810

PILOT s/ W.C. ERB (Signature)

ROUTE - MAK - MBY - DIRECT-RETURN MAK

OFFICIAL COPY(with Organizations added.)

Samuel Cutler

SAMUEL CUTLER,
Captain, Air Corps

Air transport manifest

suspended. There is a limited range, a few feet forward and aft of the wing axis, within which the location of the CG is safely allowed.

Should the aircraft become loaded beyond its CG limits, it will become unstable in flight. Improper loading of the VH-CBA airplane could have resulted in exceeding the CG limits, if its passengers had been distributed aft of the bomb-bay compartment. The CG for bombers normally is located within the bomb-bay area where its payload originally was intended to be carried. VH-CBA, however, was converted (in February 1942) from bomber to transport service.

Early in 1943, officials of the Troop Carrier Command (later named Directorate of Air Transportation) [33] became aware of the need to properly load airplane payloads and they instituted special courses of instruction.[34]

The passengers on the fatal flight were located primarily in the bomb-bay area, with some seated, toboggan-style, on the floor of the radio operator's compartment and others in the fuselage as shown in this photo.

Moreover, the passengers on these flights typically were told to squeeze-up towards the front of the plane on take-off. Such forward load distribution, most likely, did not exceeded the safe CG [center of gravity] location limits.[35]

In addition to the weight of the 35 passengers and crew of six, (200 lbs. per person), the flight's Manifest [36], recently found (April 1999) in Capt. Cutler's military files, indicates the actual figures used for calculating the weight of the aircraft, its fuel and oil load, and total payload, including one sack of mail.

The day of the final flight, the aircraft was loaded in typical mission configuration and within maximum gross weight for takeoff. The taxi weight was calculated on the manifest to be 46,810 pounds. On board were 7,200 pounds of fuel and forty-one passengers and crew. The figures closely correspond to the maximum safe weight of 47,500 lbs., cited in the Boeing Flight Manual for model B-17C. Thus the aircraft was technically not overloaded, but very close to it.[37]

Former members of the 46th Troop Carrier Squadron insist that the aircraft was not overloaded. They claim that the same VH-CBA had made many flights between Australia and New Guinea with forty men on board.[38] unfortunately, on the final flight, there is grim evidence the aircraft was incapable of gaining altitude, or of maintaining its flying speed after liftoff, on fewer than four properly operating engines. In addition, several cases of Bully Beef — not accounted for on the manifest — were found at the crash site. Apparently, the heavily loaded plane had little margin for safety.[39]

The pre-flight data gleaned from the manifest indicates that the pilots were aware of the airplane's weight limitations. It must be assumed, however, that the plane's crew also knew about the need for aerodynamic balance, assigning the passengers to floor seating locations accordingly. Nevertheless, the center of gravity could have shifted aft, if some passengers moved rearward in the plane soon after takeoff to visit the "relief-tube" urinal located in the tail section.

Another reason for exceeding the aircraft "CG limits" could have been an unexpected movement of unrestrained passengers thrust by rapid acceleration to the rear of the airplane during takeoff or the initial climbing phase of the flight. A tail-heavy condition can cause a serious loss of airspeed, reducing the aircraft's rate of climb. However, the so-called "inertia effect" is considered an unlikely problem for this type of aircraft.

The lone survivor, Cpl. Foye K. Roberts, years later said that it appeared to him that each passenger was loaded with "goodies" unobtainable in New Guinea. Besides the addition weight, the place where the purported goodies were stowed could have made a difference in the location of the "CG," especially if bags were placed in the aft section near the entrance door where most of those aboard entered the aircraft.[40] Under such circumstances, the unstable airplane resulting from the rearward shift of the CG could also have challenged the pilots.

Scenario C - Engine Fire Emergency

Eyewitnesses reported seeing flames shooting out of the low-flying plane. One saw, "a plume of flame come out of the exhaust -- as if from a flamethrower." [42]

A 1945 post-war editorial in the local newspaper, describing the [Flying Fortress] air crash of 14 June 1943, stated:

> The plane caught fire seen after taking off from Mackay aerodrome, the flames licking along the fuselage and across the wings, so that the mighty airliner appeared for a few moments as a terrifying fiery cross in the air as it screeched low towards Baker's Creek. [43]

If a fire were observed by a crewmember in any one of the four engines just after take-off, the pilot would have been faced with three problems: 1) emergency crew coordination, 2) extinguishing the engine fire, and 3) expediting a return to the airfield under conditions of reduced power, low altitude, and poor visibility. Another possible cause of fire may have been a fuel leak in one of the wings. A new fuel tank had recently been installed inside the left wing and flight-tested the previous day.

Scenario D - Engine Power Failure

An on-board emergency, such as engine or propeller failure, is another reason the pilot might attempt an immediate return to the airfield following takeoff. The greatest stress on an aircraft engine occurs during takeoff because that is the only time the throttles are up against the firewall. [44]

Retired CMSgt. Teddy W. Hanks, a former AAF aircraft mechanic and crew chief stationed near Port Moresby, New Guinea, during WW II,corresponded with two Australian civilians who observed the ill-fated Flying Fortress's final flight. Both reported seeing abnormally bright and excessively long exhaust flames coming from a starboard (right side) engine. Also, they both reported hearing loud and sharp noises, one described as "back-firing."

In addition, a local woman, who said she was standing nearer tothe aircraft's flight path and crash site than the other two eyewitnesses, described another sound coming from the low-flying B-17, as the aircraft came closer to her location. The unusual sound she heard — a propeller running in full-low pitch — was indicative of a runaway propeller, racing at extremely high RPM (engine speed).[45]

A propeller going into full "low-pitch" results from either a loss of engine oil pressure, a loss of engine power, or from a combination of the two. If the engine throttle control is put in the "full-forward" position, as during a takeoff roll, the engine RPM will be extremely high.

Chief Hanks recently wrote: (in Feb. 2001)

> The fact that B-17C (VH-CBA) performed satisfactorily the day before the crash cannot absolve its four engines of blame. Trouble-free operation one day does not guarantee continued proper operation any more than a report of good health today eliminates the possibility of a fatal heart attack tomorrow.
>
> I don't believe the maintenance crew should feel any guilt for the aircraft's fateful crash. I do believe, however, that those prone to accept the "pilot error" theory as cause of the tragedy are doing a grievous and unfounded injustice to the pilot and copilot. They were faced with unpredictable, insurmountable problems yet fought valiantly to overcome it. The fact their efforts were in vain should not detract from their valor.[46]

An aircraft engine can fail in flight for various reasons. As with any mechanical device, an internal combustion-reciprocating piston engine will fail when subjected to great stress. For the Wright Cyclone (R-1850) 9-cylinder radial engine used on the B-17C, the greatest stress usually occurs during a heavy-loaded takeoff. However, without benefit of an Engine Teardown Report, any attempt to identify the specific cause of internal engine failure remains speculative.

To maintain aircraft in operational readiness in 1943 Australia, essential parts often were removed from one airplane, or obtained from airplane graveyards, to keep another one flight-worthy. Spare engines were extremely scarce and re-supply from the U.S. was slow. An obsolete airplane would have been used for spare parts. However, by this time in the war, all other B-17C and D-model aircraft in the Southwest Pacific had been sent back to the United States.[47]

Although the Mackay police report states only that "the Flying Fortress was grounded at Mackay for the purpose of having new petrol tanks fitted,"[48] the work performed was more than the replacement of fuel tanks. Two engines needed to be replaced. Further, the plane had not been flown for nearly a month. And it was not clear whether any action was taken to preserve the condition of the remaining two engines during that time.

The 46th TCS maintenance crew assigned to the Mackay civilian airport actually installed and tested three replacement engines, in order to get two suitable ones. One test flight for the first two engines lasted about 30 minutes; they each overheated and the oil pressure dropped off. The pilot feathered the propellers and landed the plane. Once on the ground, according to former flight mechanic, Paul L. Maynard:

> I removed the magnetic oil-sump plugs on each engine; found them both full of small pieces of metal. This is a common sign of bad engine bearings. The engineering officer was finally able to obtain two new replacement engines, received in crates from the U.S., not ones rebuilt in Australia.[49]

Even though a successful flight test was performed the day before the crash, the reliability of the "brand-new" engines is highly suspect. With the failure of any one of the four engines after takeoff, the pilots would have been faced with the problem of expediting a safe return to the airfield. From the above accounts, it appears reasonable to consider that "engine power failure" is a strong contender for the probable cause of the crash.

Scenario E - Pilot's Proficiency

The aircraft was observed making two 90-degree left-turns at a low altitude. It was speculated that the pilot might have lost visual contact with the ground and possibly not fully transitioned to his instruments.[50] Further, the 46th TCS engineering officer testified to the Mackay police that takeoff was shortly after 5:58 a.m. and that "first-light" broke at 6:10 am.[51] Therefore, one can conclude the takeoff took place in early predawn darkness. In addition, local ground-fog was reported by the AAF Weather Service at 200-250 feet deep, within a few miles of the airport. The runway lights were operating normally and, according to people familiar with the Mackay airfield, the daily takeoff pattern for VH-CBA was from Runway 230, toward the southwest. A short time later, the usual flight plan would take the plane through a series of climbing left-turns in order to take up a northerly course from Mackay -- out over the Coral Sea -- toward its destination, Port Moresby, New Guinea.

On the fateful day, it is surmised, the two pilots would have had to penetrate the semi-darkness and ground fog shortly after lifting off the lighted runway; the pilot operating the controls "in the blind" until the airplane broke into clear air at an altitude of about 250 feet. This would have been their first opportunity for visual contact with the surroundings, if the plane was climbing normally. It would also be time for the landing "gear-up" flag to appear. Moreover, at least one of the two pilots should have remained on instruments until sunrise, but it is not clear whether either pilot had the necessary training. Instrument flight training had not yet been provided to DAT pilots by the Fifth Air Force. [50]

It is possible that the two low-altitude turning maneuvers were contributing factors to the crash. The second 90-degree turn may well have decreased the necessary flying speed to the degree that the heavily loaded airplane stalled and pilots lost control. This scenario for "possible cause" appears valid, so long as the pilots were not also dealing with an on-board emergency, like a fire or engine power failure. Under such critical circumstances, however, they may have properly attempted a return to the airfield at low altitude because, after making the two level turns, they realized the heavily loaded aircraft was unable to climb any higher. With loss of power from one (or two) of the four engines, just after takeoff, the pilot most probably was attempting a return to Runway 230 -- the one he just left -- particularly under the reported weather conditions of light wind and low visibility.

The Mackay Police report [51] states that just before the second 90-degree left turn at an altitude of 150 feet, the pilot was attempting to orient himself with objects on the ground in preparation for landing. One witness reported that the ground was brightly illuminated by the lights from the airplane. And another said that the aircraft was "very brightly lit from illumination attachments on the plane." [52] Apparently they were describing the beams from the high intensity landing lights housed in the leading edge of each wing.

Delmer L. Sparrowe, a World War II member of the 46th Troop Carrier Squadron, recently recounted:

> In 1943, I flew many times with the pilot, 1/Lt. Gidcumb, on B-17C (VH-CBA) out of Mackay. I also flew with Flight Officer Erb, the copilot, who had only a few flights as copilot in the B-17C. At the time, the age of most pilots in the [46th TCS] squadron was between 21 and 24 years.[53]

Because Capt. Slingsby, VH-CBA's first and most experienced pilot, returned to the United States in late March 1943, it is believed that neither his copilot, 1/Lt. Gidcumb, or F/O Erb, had more than 300 hours of flying time in multi-engine aircraft.

It must be remembered, too, that VH-CBA sat on the ground for maintenance at Mackay Airport nearly a month prior to its fatal flight while undergoing major repairs. Furthermore, since it was the only B-17C left in the 317th Troop Carrier Group, the two pilots had no opportunity to fly or remain proficient in this particular type of aircraft.

Most pilots in the Directorate of Air Transportation (DAT) at the time were fresh flying school graduates with only a few hundred flying-hours experience and limited instrument flying technique.

Because several B-24s of the 90th Bomb Group, including the one piloted by the Group commander, Colonel Art Meehan, got lost at night returning to Australia from Rabaul on November 15, 1942,

General Kenney ordered the whole 90th Group out of combat and put on training status, until they had learned night flying and navigation.[54] An extensive training course was later introduced (August 1943) by DAT, giving pilots comprehensive instruction in instrument flying.[55]

Discussion

At this late date, there is little possibility of learning the precise cause of the crash. Neither official US Army investigation reports nor engine teardown reports have been found. Nevertheless, after analyzing the information recently gathered and presented above, we believe the B-17C (VH-CBA) air crash was not caused simply by pilot error, but by a series of unfortunate events.

Routinely, the departing VH-CBA aircraft would fly back over the field and fix its position directly overhead, in order to take up a northerly course previously planned by the navigator for the 4 1/2-hour, overwater flight to Port Moresby. However, on this day, and for some reason, the pilot initiated the first 90-degree left turn at about 250 feet. After he made the second left turn, there was little margin left for error. Normally, the aircraft would climb to a 500-foot altitude before making its first 90-degree turn.

Consideration of the cause ought not to be confined to the limited observations of untrained witnesses at the crash scene who reported to police investigators — "the pilot was flying the airplane at an insufficient altitude."[56] Obviously, the old, war-torn Flying Fortress would be *at a low altitude* just before it crashed.

There are other contributing factors to consider. They include:

> the heavily loaded aircraft; the reliability of VH-CBA's battle-weary airframe; and the acknowledged training limitations among her young flight crew and maintenance personnel.[57]

Apparently some unexpected engine malfunction happened during the critical moments just before or after takeoff that prevented the airplane from climbing to its proper pattern altitude of 500 feet. Then, after leveling off, and completing its second 90-degree left-turn, the aircraft continued to lose altitude, finally crashing into a stand of trees on the Harris' paddock, five-miles short of the Mackay airport.

14

Conclusions

The cause of the crash remains uncertain, although sabotage, pilot error and poor visibility originally were claimed. The present research suggests the high probability of aircraft mechanical problems. However, now sixty years after the event, it is not possible to determine a single cause for the crash.

The accident, we now believe, was engendered by several factors, not solely because the pilot was flying the plane too low, a conclusion suggested in the Mackay Police report. Obviously, just before it crashed the plane was too low, but what circumstances brought the airplane to that place?

Review Group Comments

In December 2000, six Air Force flying veterans [58] were asked to review the available facts about the B-17C Bakers Creek air crash and provide comments. Each was later polled for his opinion regarding the probable cause. Fortunately, they were willing to reflect on their own experience, albeit for some it was nearly 60-years after the fact, to shed some light on the circumstances leading to the tragic accident.

Their comments focused on airplane loading, pilots' experience, mechanical problems, ground witness reports, weather conditions, and demands of the wartime situation.

The veterans noted that:

> That the original pre-dawn takeoff was delayed for 30-minutes, then cleared by AAF operations officer as daylight approached.
>
> That the plane had a new fuel tank and two new engines installed and satisfactory passed a flight test the previous day — unloaded and in clear daylight;

> That one witness on the ground said she saw flames, heard backfiring noises, sounds of a runaway prop;
>
> That both pilots were inexperienced with in-flight emergencies in this airplane;
>
> That several cases of Bully Beef, not accounted for on the preflight Manifest, were found in the plane wreckage — the plane may have been overloaded.
>
> That mechanics were having trouble with Australian rebuilt engines had to get two new ones from USA.
>
> That sabotage was ruled out in the Mackay police report.

One former pilot stated:

> The resulting crash was probably caused either by the gradual descent unavoidable due to loss of power or by an inadvertent descent into the trees, due to the pilots' failure to cope with the above challenges. And the weather was a factor.

A former maintenance crewmember said:

> We named that B-17C airplane, *Miss EMF,* meaning, "Every Morning Fix-It." For every eight hours of flying, we spent at least 12-hours fixing her up — usually all night long. Maintenance facilities were primitive; some of the gear we used was improvised. Lack of training and experience were factors.

And a former crew chief wrote:

> Many replacement engines supplied to flying organizations in the Southwest Pacific in 1943 were rebuilt by local AAF Depot Repair facilities in the area. Those units suffered the same inadequacies experienced by most other wartime units; patriotic and eager young men compelled to do a job for which they were inadequately trained. Obliged to reuse marginally acceptable components — such as bearings — possibly installed by marginally qualified technicians, it becomes apparent that some rebuilt engines were time bombs waiting to explode.

A contributing factor to the crash was the heavy load abroad the aircraft. The plane did be come airborne with such a load, but there is grim evidence that it was incapable of gaining altitude or maintaining flying speed on less than four properly operating engines. The heavily loaded aircraft, therefore, was denied any margin for safety.

Regarding statements in the Mackay Police report, the group was split. A minority weighed in on the "pilot error" allegation, while a majority supported the "overloading" and "mechanical problem" theories. However, all mentioned that the unfortunate combination of all of these operational factors probably caused the crash.

Finally, another reviewer wrote:

> *The truth may never be known, but we offer our hope that we have done no disservice to the memory of those who gave their lives.*

In summary, I believe that some in-flight malfunction of at least one of the four engines was the probable cause. In addition, the heavy gross weight of the airplane, poor local weather conditions and the inexperience of the pilots and the maintenance crews were also contributing factors.

This is probably the closest we shall ever come to knowing all the causes of this tragic wartime accident.

The conclusion above is based on an analyses of the information obtained from what I believe to be reliable sources in the United States and in Australia. The opinions expressed are my own and the other individuals identified and do not necessarily reflect the views of the U.S. Air Force, the Royal Australian Air Force, the Mackay City council, or of any other governmental organization.

Endnotes

1. Historical Record, Fifth Air Force, 54th Troop Carrier Wing, 317th Troop Carrier Group, 46th Troop Carrier Squadron, 1 January 1943 to 31 January 1944,(SECRET) [Declassified, DOD Dir. 5200.9, 27Sep58],68-69.

2. Foye K. Roberts, letter to Ronald and Faye (Harris) Cole, August 27, 1969.

3. Jess Rogers, statements to newspaper reporter, "Earth-Shuddering Crash Signaled Plane Tragedy," *The Daily Mercury*, May 11, 1992, 4.

4. Jim Neill, interview with Colin E. Benson, December 16, 1993, *The Daily Mercury*, December 17, 1993.

5. Pat Carroll, statement to newspaper reporter, "Witness Recalls 1943 Fortress Crash," *The Daily Mercury*, November 22, 1991, 3.

6. Historical Record, Fifth Air Force, 54th Troop Carrier Wing, 317th Troop Carrier Group, 46th Troop Carrier Squadron, 1 January 1943 to 31 January 1944, (SECRET) [Declassified, DOD Dir. 5200.9, 27 Sep. 58], 68-69.

7. Historical Record, Headquarters 317th Troop Carrier Group, Vol. l, Narration & Appendix A & B, 1 January 1943 to 31 January 1944, (SECRET) [Declassified, DOD Dir. 5200.9, 27 Sep. 58] 19-20.

8. Arnold Bragg stated to Mackay Police that he watched the plane flying east after a left banking turn, and noticed it disappear in the trees and subsequently burst into flames. He ran over immediately and searched amongst the blazing debris for possible survivors. He found two men still living [Cpl. Metzger and Cpl. Roberts].One had a badly fractured skull, the other with no indication of injury beyond a slight trickle of blood from the mouth. Bragg placed Cpl. Metzger, who was breathing torturously and remained unconscious, in a comfortable position. He then turned to Cpl. Roberts, who was lying on his stomach, and rolled him on his back. As he did so, Roberts opened his eyes. Bragg told him to lie still and went to again assist the more seriously injured man. As he was doing so, he glanced up and saw Roberts had risen to his feet and was staggering about, groaning. Mr. Bragg assisted him to a recumbent position, and had Mrs. Harris hold him thus, until the Mackay ambulance and the US Army ambulances arrived. [Arnold Radcliffe Bragg, crash scene testimony, Queensland Police Department Report, 16 June 1943, 2.]

The US Army Rest Area's medical officer, Major Siegel, attended both injured men before they were removed to the Mackay District Hospital. However, the more seriously injured man (Corporal Marlin D. Metzger) died enroute, his injuries being of such nature that Major Siegel said there was no chance of survival.

For Cpl. Foye Roberts, with the exception of some bruises and extreme shock, he sustained no apparent injury and it was considered that he would recover. Apparently his fall was cushioned by the bodies of the other men in the rear portion of the plane, all of whom were killed. He was the only man left alive of the forty-one; the six members of the crew and the 35 Army personnel [aboard the plane] when it left Mackay. [Mackay Police Dept. Report, 16 June 1943]

9. Colin E. Benson, letter to H. Brownstein, October 11, 1993.

10. Capt. Samuel Cutler, personal diary entry, June 14, 1943.

11. Robert F. Dorr, "Deadly WWII Crash Kept Quiet," History in Blue, *Air Force Times*, June 12, 2000, 12

12. Harry Moore, "We Share Their Grief," Editorial, *Mackay Daily Mercury*, June 15, 1943.

13. Colin E. Benson, letter to H. Brownstein, October 11, 1993.

14. R. Costantine, letter to R. Cutler, October 19, 1995.

15. *Ibid*

16. Capt. Samuel Cutler, personal diary entries, June 13–14, 1943.

17. *Ibid*, June 15-17, 1943

18. Mary Tileston, sister of VH-CBA's crew radio operator, Sgt. David E. Tileston, was a wartime member of the US Army's Womens Army Corps (WAC). She died shortly after the war. His twin brother, Peter Tileston, was recently contacted in Palo Alto, California, in December 2002.

19. Capt. Samuel Cutler, personal diary, June 18-25, 1943

20. *Ibid*, June 26 - July 1, 1943

21. A. N. Brooks, "Doubt About Cause of B-17C Crash," letter to editor, *The Daily Mercury*, September 9, 1999.

22. Terry Hayes, "Air Crash Story Still to be Told," *The Daily Mercury*, August 28, 1999, 2.

23. Committee members included: Rodney Manning, then editor of *The Daily Mercury*, Edmund Casey, Parliament Member for Mackay, and Mrs. Pamela Jaenke, secretary.

24. Terry Hayes, *op cit*, August, 28, 1999.

25. "Aeroplane Crash: Flying Fortress VHCBA at Bakers Creek via Mackay," Mackay District Queensland Police Department, 16 June 1943.

26. Cover letter, C.J. Carroll, Commissioner of Police, Qld., to Brigadier-General Donaldson, US Army SWPA, APO 923, dtd. 26 June 1943. Acknowledged by 2/Lt. R.W. Bolling, Actg. Asst. Adjutant General, Office of the Commanding General, Headquarters, Base Section 3, USASOS, APO 923, dtd. 4 July 1943.

> Report which you forwarded (Reference No. 1861M.93 26 June 1943) has been noted and forwarded to the Commanding General, Fifth Air Force, for information. The co-operation of The Queensland Police Force in this matter and in many others is appreciated, as are your expressions of sympathy in this tragic occurrence. [2/Lt. R.W. Bolling, Actg. Asst. Adj. Gen., USASOS, 4 July 1943]

27. Senior Sergeant C. Howie, Inspector of Police, endorsement to report, "Aeroplane Crash: Flying Fortress VHCBA at Bakers Creek via Mackay," Mackay District Queensland Police Department, June 16, 1943, 6.

28. Teddy W. Hanks, letter to R. Cutler, February 6, 2001.

29. Colin E. Benson, Terry Hayes, Edmund D. Casey,(Australia) and Teddy W. Hanks, Herbert S. Brownstein, Robert S. Cutler (United States).

30. Historical Record, 317th Troop Carrier Group, Volume I, 1 January 1943 – 31 January 1944, 19, and Historical Record, 46th Troop Carrier Squadron, 317th Troop Carrier Group, Fifth Air Force, 1 January 1943 – 31 January 1944, 68-69.

31. R. Costantine and D. Sparrowe, interview with R. Cutler at the 46th TCS Reunion, Louisville, KY, Sept. 30, 2000.

32. Dewey Walker, a former S/Sgt.mechanic with 46th TCS who helped change engines and fuel tank days preceding the crash of B-17C (VH-CBA), comments in *The Daily Mercury,* May 11, 1992, 3.

> Although the [Flying Fortress - 40-2072] had beenin service for a considerable time, two of its fourengines were new and the other two had only 100 hours of flying time.

33. History of the Directorate of Air Transport, 322nd Troop Carrier Wing, 13.

34. *Ibid*,16

35. R. Costantine, conversation with H. Brownstein. 1997.

36. Air Transport Control Manifest, B-17C (VH-CBA),(true copy) Capt. Samuel Cutler, Executive Officer, US Army Rest Area, Mackay, June 14, 1943.

37. Technical Order, B-17C (01-20EC-1), December 11, 1941, 48.

38. R. Costantine and D. Sparrowe, interview with R. Cutler, 46th TCS Reunion, Louisville, KY, September 30, 2000.

39. Teddy W. Hanks, "The Bakers Creek Air Crash," unpublished technical narrative, Feb. 6, 2001.

40. Teddy W. Hanks, letter to R. Cutler, Feb. 16, 2001

41. *Ibid*

42. Teddy W. Hanks, "The Bakers Creek Aircraft Crash," Technical Narrative (unpublished), January 6, 2000

43. *The Daily Mercury*, August 21, 1945

44. Teddy W. Hanks, letter to R. Cutler, Feb 16, 2001

45. *Ibid*

46. *Ibid*

47. Herbert S. Brownstein, *The Swoose*, Washington DC: Smithsonian Institution Press, 1992, 20.

48. Mackay Police Report, "Aeroplane Crash: Flying Fortress VHCBA at Bakers Creek, via Mackay," Mackay District Queensland Police Department, 16 June 1943, 2.

49. Paul L. Maynard, email to R. Cutler, Nov. 16, 2000.

50. Before America's entry into the war, little had been done to teach fledgling Army Air Force pilots the rudiments of instrument flying. Student pilots were taught to use only three basic flight instruments for all-weather navigation: airspeed indicator, altimeter, and turn and bank indicator. The gyroscopic turn indicator and artificial horizon were neglected. Instrument flying time required for graduation from pilot school amounted to 15-20 hours. [Samuel Fishbein, *Flight Management*, Westport CT: Praeger, 1995, 17]

51. Mackay Police Report, *op cit*, 4.

52. Cyril Victor Godwin, testimony to Police investigator, Queensland Police Report, "Aeroplane Crash: Flying Fortress VHCBA at Bakers Creek via Mackay," Mackay District Queensland Police Department, 16 June 1943, 6.

53. Delmer L. Sparrowe, email message to R. Cutler, Feb.12,2001.

54. A comprehensive program of instrument flying instruction was introduced to pilots of the Fifth Air Force in 1943. [George C. Kenney, *General Kenney Reports: A Personal History of the Pacific War*, New York: Duell, Sloan and Pearce, 1949, 125].

55. Samuel Fishbein, *Flight Management*, 17

56. Lt. Eugene Neighbors, testimony to police investigator, Queensland Police Report, "Aeroplane Crash: Flying Fortress VHCBA at Bakers Creek via Mackay," Mackay District Queensland Police Department, 16 June 1943, 4.

57. Delmer L. Sparrowe, Email message to R. Cutler, Feb. 12, 2001.

58. Reviewers were: Lt. Gen. John B. Hall, Jr., USAF (Ret.); Lt. Col. H. James Greene, USAF (Ret.); CMSgt. Teddy W. Hanks, USAF (Ret.); Delmer L. Sparrowe, former S/Sgt., 46th TCS; Romeo "Connie" Costantine, former S/Sgt., 46th TCS; and Paul L. Maynard, former Sgt., 46th TCS.

PART 3

The Rememberence

Queen Street, City of Mackay in 1943

15

Mackay Remembers

Having chronicled the history of B-17C Flying Fortress (40-2072) in Section I (The Airplane), and presented an analysis of the technical details of the crash in Section II (The Air Crash), we focus attention now on the monument built to honor the ill-fated crew, the 35 passengers and the only survivor. Their names are now inscribed on the Bakers Creek Memorial, near Mackay, in North Queensland, Australia.[1]

The tragedy shocked the local Mackay community. Many had known members of the crew and several families had befriended a few of the passengers during their stay in Mackay on furlough. They had just hosted many of these young Americans in their homes and at nearby recreation facilities. It seemed like members of their own families had perished in the fiery early morning explosion.

US Army officials in Mackay kept the local people away from the crash site, suppressing publicity about the incident. However, Harry Moore, editor of *The Daily Mercury*, managed to publish a small, veiled editorial expressing sorrow about the tragic loss.[2]

US Army Rest Area

In the later months of 1942, it became apparent that the Allied forces had established a firm foothold in the southeastern portion of New Guinea, and the ground and air battles increased. It was also apparent to Lt. General George C. Kenney, the commander of the Fifth Air Force, that a program was desperately needed whereby battle-weary ground personnel in combat units based on the island could be sent south to Australia for short periods of rest and recuperation. Many were sick and becoming malnourished. Since a

The Bakers Creek Memorial honours the sole survivor and 40 American servicemen who lost their lives when LGAAF B-17C Flying Fortress #40-2072 crashed at Bakers Creek, soon after take off from Mackay airport at 6.02am on Monday 14th June 1943.

Col Benson photo

"Early yesterday morning Floyd K. Roberts (ZZ) a visiting serviceman was taken to the District Hospital from Bakers Creek by the ambulance suffering from internal injuries"

The Daily Mercury Tuesday June 15 1943.

PERSONNEL ON BOARD

CREW

1/Lt	Vern J GIDCUMB	(Pilot)
F/O	William C ERB	(Co-Pilot)
2/Lt	Jack A. OGREN	(Navigator)
S/Sgt	Lovell Dale CURTIS	(Crew Chief)
S/Sgt	Frank E WHELCHEL	(Crew Chief)
Sgt	David E TILESTON	(Radio)

PASSENGERS

Pfc	Jerome Abraham	Capt	John O BETHOLD
T/5	William A BRIGGS	Sgt	Dean H BUSSE
T/Sgt	James A COPELAND	Sgt	Carl A CUNNINGHAM
T/5	George A. EHRMAN	Pvt	James E FINNEY
Sgt	Leo E FLETCHER	T/Sgt	Alfred H FREZZA
Pfc	Norman J GOETZ	S/Sgt	Roy A HATLEN
S/Sgt	John W HILSHEIMER	Pfc	Vernon JOHNSON
Sgt	Donald B KYPER	Sgt	Charlie O L:ARUE
Pvt	Raymond D LONGBAUGH	Pfc	Kenneth W MANN
Pvt	Marlin D METZGER	Pvt	Charles D MONTGOMERY
Pfc	John W PARKER	Pfc	Frank S PENSKA
Maj	George N POWELL	Sgt	Anthony RUDNICK
Cpl	Charles W SAMPSON	Pfc	Arnold SEIDEL
Cpl	Jacob O SKAGGS	Cpl	Franklin F SMITH
Cpl	Raymond H SMITH	Pfc	Frederick C SWEET
Cpl	Edward TENNY	Pfc	Dale VAN FOSSON
Pvt	Ruben L VAUGHN	Pfc	Charles M WILLIAMS

SURVIVOR

Sgt Foye K. ROBERTS

Lest We Forget

Bakers Creek Memorial Card

program enabling officers on flying status to take leave in Sydney had been in effect for a number of months, General Kenney proposed a similar one for his non-flying officers and enlisted men.[2]

The project was assigned to the Army's Services of Supply (USASOS) staff in Brisbane. Those assigned the task of selecting a location for a rest area had to consider several criteria: the site had to be far enough removed from the combat zone to assure complete safety from enemy attacks, yet close enough to preclude lengthy travel time. The site must be sufficiently removed from an existing military facility so that a civilian rather than a military atmosphere would prevail. The weather must be compatible with the summer uniform, the only attire available to those in New Guinea. The site must have ample housing facilities, pleasant recreational facilities, local inhabitants who would gladly accept military visitors, and a nearby airport that would accommodate large transport aircraft. Mackay easily met those requirements.

The American Red Cross Center

Early in 1943, the US Army and the American Red Cross established a jointly operated R&R (rest and recreation) center in Mackay. This tropical seaside resort town, located 600 miles north of Brisbane along the Great Barrier Reef, was only four and one—half hours of B-17 flying time due south across the Coral Sea from Port Moresby, New Guinea, and away from the advancing enemy. Primarily reserved for enlisted personnel fighting the enemy in the hot, mosquito-infested jungles, the men were granted 10-days R&R leave and then returned by transport aircraft to their assigned units, located within the combat zone.

From mid-March 1943, Mackay became a major recreation center for American servicemen coming from the battlefields of New Guinea. And by three months later, in June 1943, the local citizens had become accustomed to the American GIs' presence, and also, the regular flights that carried them daily to and from their safe seaside city. It was said that you could set your clock by the arrival and the departure of the B-17's. From 4: 00 p.m. each afternoon, they would appear from the north, and at 5:30 a.m. in the morning, the roar of their four engines could be heard as they prepared for their flight northward.[3]

American Red Cross Centre on Wood street

10-Days R&R in Mackay

The American Red Cross Center was located in the mid-town area, near the hotels and hosted rooming houses. It provided formal entertainment for the American servicemen on leave. A live band, including top-class performers like then famous radio singer, Lanny Ross, played popular wartime hits. Some luxuries, such as milk shakes, chewing gum, chocolates and ice cream were sold in a "milk-bar" style Canteen, staffed by the American Red Cross personnel. The men were also entertained by movies and group horseback riding excursions.

Courtesy The *Daily Mercury*

American servicemen on leave in Mackay enjoyed beach picnics

Moonlit beaches and hayrides also entertained the Americans. Many folks in Mackay gave "practical friendship" to these serviceman to help them enjoy their leave time in Mackay. For example, after work, local wagon drivers would hitch-up their horse teams and drive chaperoned parties of American soldiers and local girls in their farm wagons to Far Beach, a good place for evening parties and barbecues. The approach to Far Beach in those days was by a dirt road, and the hurricane lamps swinging underneath the wagons added to the cozy atmosphere. And for many Mackay residents, the American idea of a "barbecue" was something new. And it would often be nearly 3:00 a.m. before they were on their way home.

The American Red Cross Center, located in the mid-town area near the hotels and hosted rooming houses, provided the formal entertainment for the American servicemen on leave. A live band, including top-class performers like then famous radio singer, Lanny Ross, played popular wartime hits. Some luxuries, such as milk shakes, chewing gum, chocolates and ice cream were sold in a "milk-bar" style Canteen, staffed by American Red Cross personnel. The men were also entertained by movies and group horseback riding excursions.

Courtesy US Air Force History Agency

Dance held at American Red Cross Hall. Guest of honor was Lt. Lanny Ross, formerly feature singer on the Maxwell House radio program in the United States

Caption: Dance held at American Red Cross Hall. Guest of honor was Lt. Lanny Ross, formerly feature singer on the Maxwell House radio program in the United States.]

One housing facility was the former residence of a local physician, Dr. Paul Hopkins. The house provided accommodation for nearly forty servicemen. Every day, ten men left in the morning, having completed their 10-day stay, and another ten came in the late afternoon.

Local folks in Mackay knew the American soldiers by first names only; surnames never mattered. Almost everyone admired them for their cleanliness and their good behavior. One could not remember there being a fight involving the GIs during the time.

Shoeshine boys set themselves up at street corners and earned big money. A young chap who had his stand at the hospital guarded it jealously and would never let anyone work in his territory. Some of them had so much money they could bid in 5 and 10-pound notes, (US $15-$30) when playing "pitch penny" with the Americans. They played in a vacant lot opposite the Commonwealth Bank. A small circle was drawn on the ground. The object of the game was to pitch a penny coin as close to the center as possible.

Schoolboys living near the railway station were among those who welcomed the crowds of Americans passing through Mackay during the critical war years. They often would challenge to them to bicycle races along Main Street, from the Explorer's Tree to the railroad bridge -- for a small wager.

Most citizens of wartime Mackay in 1943 told the same story about the American soldiers. They were first attracted to them for their youth, their courtesy, their hominess, and for their appreciation of the kindness being offered by the Australians. This was despite tawdry incidents such as the notorious "Battle of Brisbane", in which thousands of Australian and American servicemen got into bitter clashes. Thousands of Americans passed through Mackay in 1943. Though they came to enjoy themselves, their behavior with few exceptions was exemplary. Picture shows, dances and picnics were arranged almost every night, but most of all the American soldiers liked to be invited into private homes and treated as one of the family. Touring the district on horseback or by bicycle was also a popular pastime.

Many young soldiers were trying out their horse riding ability for the first time. Their horsemanship, more enthusiastic than skilled, amused the locals highly. Nevertheless, the American boys enjoyed it and often arranged impromptu races among themselves.

A popular racecourse was from the Fire Station down Sydney Street to the Forgan Bridge. Not all of them were "greenhorns". And those men from rural backgrounds were often invited to experience daily life on a North Queensland sugarcane farm.

The GIs relished the fresh milk, cream and fruit from the local farms. They also liked the good beef, but were not too fond of mutton. There was one instance in a grocery store when an American soldier purchased a dozen cans of corned mutton. The shopkeeper commented that the troops must like Aussie mutton.

"Oh, no," the American GI said, "that's for the dawg."

Crew Members Remembered

A photo of SSgt. Dale Curtis, a crew chief on the ill-fated B-17C (VH-CBA), was left on the piano of the Frank Griffiths home on George Street in Mackay. Colin E. Benson, Mackay RSL historian who researched the matter, reports that although he was not able to recover the photo, several months later a former 46th TCS buddy (SSgt. "Connie" Costantine) sent a duplicate photo from the United States. Presumably it was the same one taken in a Mackay photo studio a few weeks before the fatal 1943 crash.

Similarly, Barney McGuire, then a teenage son of the proprietors of the McGuire's Hotel, in Mackay, where several American airmen (Sergeants Romeo "Connie" Costantine, Del Sparrowe, Paul Maynard, Dale Curtis and most of the aircrew's "noncoms") were billeted, once remarked "a photo of Dale Curtis hung in the McGuire's Hotel until the family sold the place in the 1960s."

Upon reading about the wager between two B-17 crew chiefs -- Del Sparrowe and Dale Curtis flipping a coin to determine which one would fly on the [fatal] next day's trip -- Barney McGuire thought that it was his coin. Barney's mother sold the coin to an American staying in the McGuire's Hotel. But Del Sparrowe believes that someone in another Mackay family, who befriended him by organizing his 21st birthday party in 1943, had given the coin to him.[6]

Courtesy Marylin (Curtis) Fields

SSgt Lovell Dale Curtis, 46th Troop Carrier Squadron, was flying crew chief on ill-fated Flying Fortess (VH-CBA)

16

Wartime Snapshot of Mackay

Contributed by Terence P. Hayes

Mackay, Queensland, in 1943 was a city of 12,000 people. It was an ideal haven for the men of the U.S Fifth Air Force seeking a carefree 10-days of R&R. They could be away from the grim reality of war and from the rigors of bivouac life in the rain-drenched New Guinea jungles rampant with malaria, and the even more deadly disease, scrub typhus.

From the air, Mackay presented a peaceful and attractive vista to the incoming servicemen. They could see long stretches of sandy beaches along the coastline, and further out, the coral-fringed shores of islands destined to become world-renowned tourist resorts in the post war years. The city itself was surrounded to the north, south and west by acres and acres of fertile sugar cane fields, which in June were ripe for harvest.

Mackay's larger neighboring cities, Rockhampton 200 miles to the south and Townsville 230 miles to the north, had become garrison cities in the early months of 1942. Tens of thousands of American servicemen camped on the outskirts of Rockhampton, while Townsville was packed both with American and Australian troops. It was the principal base for mounting Allied airborne attacks on Japanese strongholds in New Guinea and on the dangerous Japanese naval fleets in the Bismarck and Coral seas.

In Mackay, however, there were no great indications of military activity, other than a few American installations, such as the ship-servicing units at Mackay Harbor, four miles north of the city. Nevertheless, the men of the Fifth Air Force were coming to a community which knew well the anxiety and bitter sorrow brought by war.

In those dark months of early 1942, Mackay was well within the potential battle zone, called the “Brisbane Line”. In the face of the real threat of enemy

Courtesy Samuel L. Cutler collection

Aerial view of the City of Mackay - 1943

invasion, schools had been closed, air raid posts established, and essential Government records moved to western towns. Many private citizens also made their own evacuation plans, moving to southern or western locations. In those fearful months, heavy items of household furniture, such as pianos and bookcases, could be bought for just a few Australian pounds. ($6.50 dollars) *[Question: Is this the approx correct value, today?]

Well before the December 1941 outbreak of war with Japan, local men from Mackay had been fighting and falling in the battles of the African desert, in the doomed defense of Greece and Crete, and in naval battles of the Mediterranean Sea.

The sorrows born of casualty lists from those battles were compounded by the disastrous loss of Malaya and the surrender of Singapore on February 15, 1942. A very high proportion of Mackay soldiers were in the Australian 8th Division, which fought in the Malayan campaign. The fate of many of them still was unknown late as mid-1943. On June 9, 1943, even as those 40 American servicemen fated to die in the Flying Fortress crash a few days later were still enjoying their R&R leave, a casualty list from Malaya was published. It contained the names of four well-known local men who previously had been posted as "missing in action," but now listed as "prisoners of war" of the Japanese.

The decisive Battle of the Coral Sea, in the first week of May 1942, was followed by the defeat of a Japanese invasion force at Milne Bay on the southern tip of New Guinea on September 6, 1942. And the Australian victory in the Kokoda Trail battle, in late November 1942, eased the threat of an enemy invasion to Australia.

Australian and American bombers based in Townsville had taken part in the Battle of the Coral Sea, in which the opposing Allied and Japanese naval forces never sighted each other. Losses on both sides were about even, but the important outcome of the battle was the fact that it deterred the Japanese navy from any further full-scale incursion into the Coral Sea, which touches the coastline of North Queensland in Australia.

At the Battle of Milne Bay, the Japanese Army suffered its first major defeat. The Japanese had made a landing there intent on driving overland along the southern coast of New Guinea to Port Moresby. But after a week of bitter jungle fighting, the Australian 7th Militia Brigade and the 18th Brigade, 7th AIF Division, repelled them. Citizens Militia Forces were composed of young Australians drafted for military service, whereas the AIF Divisions were composed entirely of men who had volunteered for service.

By August 1942, the Japanese assault in southern New Guinea along the Kokoda Track reached within 40 miles of Port Moresby. There they were halted and painfully driven back, almost yard-by-yard. Kokoda fell to the Australians on November 2, 1942. Then, Gona, a Japanese northern New Guinea coastal base was captured on November 26. Finally, the combined Australian and American assault, under Lt. General Eichelberger, won the "Bloody Battle for Buna" at the end of December 1942. With the fall of those three major Japanese bases, Australia now appeared secure from enemy invasion -- and the Allied Forces were ready to go on to the attack.

By early 1943, the people of Mackay resumed a more normal wartime way of life. While Australians were justly proud of the battle proved fighting caliber of their own troops, the presence of the American servicemen, together with their powerful airplanes and equipment, brought them a welcome sense of assurance. The general feeling was that, in the end, the Allied cause would prevail and Australia would be spared the bloody torment inflicted on so many European and Asian countries.

On March 15, 1943, and with thoughts for their own boys serving overseas still close to their hearts, the people of Mackay were ready to extend Australian friendship and hospitality to the men of the US Fifth Air Force, as group by group of the battle weary young GIs arrived for their 10-days of R & R leave.

Even before the official hostels were set up, Mackay families were welcoming the Americans into their homes. One family, Sydney Street barber, Frank McKeever, his wife Lillian and their 17-year-old daughter, Frances, hosted five Americans at a time in their home in North Mackay. Lillian McKeever wrote to many American mothers to tell them that she had seen their sons and that they were well. Friendships thus made by the McKeevers and by many other families in Mackay endured for lifetimes.

By June 1943, American Red Cross facilities were well established in Mackay. The constant flow of American GIs was now an accepted as part of the city's lifestyle. The young Americans won the hearts of the community. Schoolboys were captivated by their uniforms and the sweets and tips they so freely dispersed. The young girls were enthralled by their glamour and courtesy. The mothers of families took them to their hearts because of their kindness and their concern for the older generation. And the fathers admired them for their manliness, for the important part they were playing in winning the war.

The generosity of the American visitors was boundless. In that one year of 1943, some Mackay institutions such as schools and churches were able to accumulate sufficient financial resources to see them through their building and development programs during the austere post war years. Scores of Americans could be counted upon to turn up at school or church socials and dances, many of them on bicycles. Those events were always alive with good spirits and happiness. Many of the Americans, feeling that they had no need of money in New Guinea, or even might not live long enough to spend it all, spread their money around with abandon. And they were eager, but not very shrewd, bettors at the weekly trotting and galloping events.

The American Red Cross Center (ARC) on Wood Street became the real hub of Mackay's social life. The "Britainettes", a troupe of local girls formed to perform with the ARC entertainers, became very popular there. The girls themselves retained fond memories, throughout their future lives, of the hundreds of America servicemen they got to know. (Mrs. Vera Britain, the American Red Cross worker who organized the "Britainettes", was later captured and executed by the Japanese).

Courtesy Joyce A. Graham

ARC Meeting of Air Force Victorettes with Marcille Gunther

The Americans liked to be part of the day-to-day life of Mackay. Herbert L. Patrick, the ARC director, a member of Rotary International in his hometown of Portland, Oregon, regularly attended meetings of the Rotary Club of Mackay. Before leaving the city in July 1944, he presented a United States ceremonial flag to the Mackay Rotary Club, in appreciation for the warm welcomes given to the US servicemen in Mackay, and as a symbol of friendship between the United States and Australia.

For many years the flag was cared for by Rotarian Al Soxman, an American serviceman who settled in Mackay after the war with his Mackay born wife, Nita. In 1983, the Rotary Club handed over custody of the flag to the Mackay City Council. It is one of the permanent mementoes of the Americans who came to Mackay in 1943, now held by the City Council. The other is the pine tree, now growing behind the Mackay City Library, which was used as the Christmas tree for the Americans at Christmas 1943. The tree was grown in the Council's Queen's Park plant nursery and transplanted outside the ARC Center on Wood Street in time for the 1943 Christmas celebrations in which hundreds of local people joined with the Americans.

As those US Fifth Air Force personnel, who soon were to perish at Bakers Creek, flew out of Port Moresby on their way to R&R in Mackay, their comrades still on duty in New Guinea were heavily engaged in combat against the enemy. Many USAAF airplanes were heavily engaged in several important missions along New Guinea's northern coast. On June 1, 1943, a B-17E flown by 2/Lt Henry Evans was attacked by 18 Zeros over the sea east of Finschafen. The

Fortress shot down four of the Zeros and eluded the others by diving down to a 200-foot altitude. The Fortress had then flown 31 missions, was credited with having shot down 16 Zeros. On June 10th, B-17 Fortresses and B-24 Liberators from fields in New Guinea launched heavy raids on Rabaul. They destroyed many Japanese aircraft on the ground at three airstrips. And one week earlier, US aircraft also bombed Wewak, another strong Japanese air base.

There was another reminder of the war in Mackay during the week of June 6th, when the new issue of ration books was delivered to all householders. The new rationing regulations were more stringent than those previously in force. The butter ration was further curtailed and new restrictions were placed on towels, sheets, pillow cases and tablecloths to conserve on stocks of cotton goods, all of which had been previously imported from Britain, the USA and India. The impending issue of the new ration books caused a rush on city stores by housewives eager to use up all of the current coupons. So great was the rush that most stores sold out their stocks in only four days.

While rationing was irksome and inconvenient to local residents, there was also some good news for them. An official announcement was made by Australia's Prime Minister, John Curtin, on June 10, 1943, that the danger of invasion of Australia was now past. Mr Curtin stated that he had had a conference with General Douglas Macarthur who assured him that Australia was now safe from invasion.

Unaware they were now entering their last week on earth, those American servicemen due to fly back to New Guinea on June 14th, participated in the entertainment available to them in Mackay with light hearts. There were some great films to choose from. They included: Dorothy Lamour in Beyond the Blue Horizon, Alice Faye, Don Ameche and Carmen Miranda in That Night in Rio, John Wayne in The Flying Tigers, and Laurel and Hardy in A Haunting We Will Go. And on their very last night, some of them may have laughed at the antics of Olsen and Johnson in Hellzapoppin.

Courtesy Joyce A. Graham

American sevicemen enjoying music

The American Red Cross Center arranged the usual program of recreation — horseback riding, picnics and barbecues. During the ten days they were in Mackay, there were Sunday baseball games in Queen's Park and dancing and live entertainment every night at the ARC Center. The Yank Swing Band provided the music on Friday night, June 4th, and there was another big local dance that Friday night at the Church of England Parish Hall. A local pianist, Marj Healy, led the orchestra for the Parish Hall dance and she played again at the Workers' Club dance in the Majestic Hall on Saturday night.

On their last Saturday night in Mackay, most of the doomed men were among the dancers in the ARC Center who welcomed the new band leader, Claude Carnell. Claude had come from Melbourne to take over the orchestra. With him were vocalist Enid Biddle, Graeme Bell at the piano, Des Colbert on the trumpet and Les Smith, drummer.

Some of the boys were at the boxing tournament at the Olympic Theatre on Thursday night to cheer on their countryman, Peter Rodeo. Peter, the only American fighting in the tournament, was beaten on points by a good local boxer, Tommy Sandiman.

As happened every Sunday, there was a sprinkling of Americans in the congregations at various church services on June 13th. The Church of England service was held at Holy Trinity Church at 7.00 am. Catholics attended Mass at St. Patrick's and St. Mary's, while other services were being held for Presbyterians, Methodists, and for Lutherans. The Salvation Army service was held at 3.00 pm.

Courtesy Joyce A. Graham

American servicemen and Townpeople after service at Presbyterian Church, Mackay (1943)

For most people in Mackay associated with the Americans, that fateful Monday morning, June 14, 1943, was just like any other. There were some tearful farewells on Sunday night, addresses were exchanged, and some Mackay mothers already were planning to write to the families of men who had visited in their homes.

Daybreak Departure

Dawn was just breaking as the crewmen and passengers filed into the big, dark B-17C airplane. In a remote paddock in the little farming settlement of Peri on the outskirts of the city, Jess Roger was engaged in her daily routine of rounding up the cows. She sat on her horse waiting to see the Flying Fortress take off, as she did every morning. She heard the roar of the engines warming up, then head the take off. As always happened, the plane came into view above the trees. But this time it was different. Jess Roger saw the Fortress rise to about 300 feet and then, as it made a sweep towards the southwest, she sensed that the pilot was in trouble. It seemed that he could not get the nose up. Sitting helplessly in the saddle, Jess followed the flight to disaster. The engines began backfiring, then a flash of flame illuminated the entire fuselage from cockpit to tail, the Fortress fell almost flat from the sky. There was a tremendous crash, the countryside was lit up by the brilliant flames. The ground under her, one and a half miles in a straight line from the crash site, shuddered and reverberated.

Almost within minutes ambulances and Military Police in jeeps were speeding out along Nebo Road to the crash site at Bakers Creek. Sadly all was beyond help. Wreckage of the once proud warplane was strewn everywhere. Bodies of the dead and dying lay all around, and alone.

Rudy Sabbo, a local resident, was recently interviewed by Mackay State High School teacher, Bruce Litte. He told Mr. Litte that he had been to the crash site after the crash.

> About 30 of the men were in the rear end of the fuselage stacked like pillows without a mark on them, all facing each other, side by side. There were two bench seats, one on each side of the plane. The men faced each other and had obviously slid down to the back with the crash impact. They all looked like they were sleeping.[8]

In the midst of the carnage were two men: Cpl. Marlin D. Metzger, who died en route to hospital, and the only survivor, Cpl. Foye K Roberts. They were being comforted by Mrs. Gertrude Harris (mother of Mrs. Faye Cole, now owner of Mackay's White Lace Motel), who had hurried from her farmhouse to the crash scene.

News of the disaster spread quickly throughout Mackay. Tears were shed, regrets were sorrowfully spoken and saddened hearts prayed. Then the dark veil of wartime censorship descended on the city, to shade from public view this military aviation tragedy and the brave men who had died there. The bodies of the dead were flown to Townsville for temporary burial in the Belgian Gardens Cemetery, and years later after the war, many were returned to the United States to rest finally among the homeland of their youth. Six pieces of the wreckage salvaged from the site are now held in the Mirani Shire Council Museum, 22 miles from Mackay.

Memories Endure

The passage of 60 years has not dimmed the warmth of Mackay's feeling for the thousands of American servicemen to whom it was once home for 10 days. The Americans bought a new life and enjoyment to wartime Mackay, they gave the local people a glimpse into a larger world, once unknown to them.

Mackay became a better place because of their presence.

* * *

Terrence P. Hayes is a local Mackay journalist and historian who regularly researches and writes local history articles for The Daily Mercury. *As a young man, he visited the crash site on bicycle and grew up in the area knowing personally about the Flying Fortress aviation tragedy in WW II. Over the years, he has penned many articles about the Bakers Creek air crash.*

17

The List of Casualties

When the Bakers Creek Air Crash Memorial was dedicated on May 11, 1992, only the names of the six crewmembers and the sole survivor were known. Then, Colin E. Benson, a retired Vietnam-era RAAF Warrant Officer and the historian of the Mackay Branch of the Returned Services League of Australia (RSL), decided to take up a search for the full casualty list.

Courtesy Colin E. Benson

Colin E. Benson, Mackay RSL Historian

Benson wrote a letter to an acquaintance at the Franklin Institute of Science, in Philadelphia, Pennsylvania, which was forwarded to uS Air Force retiree, CMSgt. Teddy W. Hanks, in Texas.[9] Hanks then wrote back to Colin Benson, in late 1993, telling him that he had a listing of some 52 names, but felt it was the responsibility of the US Army's Total Personnel Center's (TAPC) to provide him with the correct listing of the crash victims, since he had made and officially request for them. But finally, Hanks agreed to send his tentative listing, which included the name of a Captain Berthold, whom he believed was <u>not</u> one of the Bakers Creek crash victims.

Chief Hanks had lost four of his friends in the crash. And he knew all too well how many of the vicitms' families suffered their losses. In an email exchange with me, Ted Hanks wrote:

> When I personally talk with one of those who suffered a loss at Bakers Creek, I'm further convinced that what we are doing not only is right — it is necessary. It's truly a sad, very sad, thing that so many families down through the years have wondered and agonized about what exactly happened to their loved ones.

> Being one who has stood close, eyeball-to-eyeball, with the Grim Reaper
>
> on a couple of occasions and survived the ordeal, *I now know why the Good Lord has let me live.*" [10]

In the March 1994 issue of *American Legion Magazine*, Hanks placed a small notice regarding the B-17C crash in Australia in 1943. He received several phone calls. One was from a former 49th Fighter Group enlisted man who confirmed that Captain John O. Berthold was indeed a Bakers Creek crash victim. Capt. Berthold, a non-flying officer, was the Adjutant of the 8th Fighter Squadron of the 49th Fighter Group. That unit lost six men in the crash, including the only two officers riding as passengers. The other officer, Major George W. Powell, at age 52, was the oldest man on the plane.

Search for Names

Ted Hanks continued his search for the full list of casualties. Since the "Historic Reports of the 317th Troop Carrier Group" for 1943 revealed no passenger lists, he then wrote to several veterans' groups and to the American Red Cross. No response from any of them. A few months later, Hanks wrote to the US National Archives in Washington, DC, also not expecting a favorable reply. To his surprise, within a month's time he received a letter stating:

Courtesy Robert S. Cutler

Teddy W. Hanks, CMSgt. USAF (Ret.)

> We have searched the records of the Office of the US Army Quartermaster General and located a weekly report of burials, dated 28 June 1943, which includes the men buried in the temporary Townsville BelgianGardens Cemetery on 18 June 1943. [11]

Finally, after nearly three years, *he had hit pay dirt!*

The Casualty List

Shown on the following page are the names, ranks, organizations, and final burial sites of the forty crash victims.

CASUALTIES OF THE USAAF B-17C FLYING FORTRESS S/No. 40-2072 CRASH AT BAKERS CREEK, NEAR MACKAY, QUEENSLAND, ON 14 JUNE 1943.

NAME	RANK	UNIT	FINAL RESTING PLACE
ABRAHAM, Jerome	Pfc	49th FG, HQ Sqn	FLORIDA
BERTHOLD, John O.	Capt	49th FG, 8th FS	NEW YORK , Woodlawn National Cemetery, Elmira
BRIGGS, William A.	T/5	478th SS, 1037th Sig	HAWAII, National Memorial Cemetery of the Pacific, Honolulu
BUSSE, Dean H.	Sgt	35th FG, 40th FS,	COLORADO, Hillside Cemetery, Julesburg
COPELAND, James A.	T/Sgt	8th SG, HQ Sqn	HAWAII, National Memorial Cemetery of the Pacific, Honolulu
CUNNINGHAM, Carl A.	Sgt	49th FG, 8th FS	HAWAII, National Memorial Cemetery of the Pacific, Honolulu
CURTIS, Lovell Dale (Crew Chief)	S/Sgt	317th Troop CG, 46th TCS	HAWAII, National Memorial Cemetery of the Pacific, Honolulu
EHRMAN, George A.	T/5	5th FC, Sig HQ Co	CALIFORNIA, Golden Gate National Cemetery, San Bruno
ERB, William C. (Co-Pilot)	F/O	317th Troop CG, 46th TCS	CALIFORNIA
FINNEY, James E.	Pvt	27th DRS	PENNSYLVANIA
FLETCHER, Leo E.	Sgt	38th BG, 405th BS	KENTUCKEY
FREZZA, Alfred H.	T/Sgt	27th DRS	PENNSYLVANIA (Altoona?)
GIDCUMB, Vern J. Jr. (Pilot)	1/Lt	317th Troop CG, 46th TCS	ILLINOIS, Wolf Creek Cemetery, Eldorado
GOETZ, Norman J.	Pfc	480th SS	ILLINOIS, St. Mary's Cemetery, Evergreen Park
HATLEN, Roy A.	S/Sgt	35th FG, 40th FS	HAWAII, National Memorial Cemetery of the Pacific, Honolulu
HILSHEIMER, John W.	S/Sgt	35th FG, 40th FS	Unknown (Arlington indicated in records - not buried there)
JOHNSON, Vernon	Pfc	440th Sig Bn, Co A	HAWAII, National Memorial Cemetery of the Pacific, Honolulu
KYPER, Donald B.	Sgt	38th BG, 405th BS	PENNSYLVANIA, Riverview Cemetery, Huntingdon
LaRUE, Charlie O.	Sgt	49th FG, 8th FS	HAWAII, National Memorial Cemetery of the Pacific, Honolulu
LONGABAUGH, Raymond D.	Pvt	842nd Aviation Eng Bn	HAWAII, National Memorial Cemetery of the Pacific, Honolulu
MANN, Kenneth W.	Pfc	36th SG, 374th SS	MISSOURI, Jefferson City National Cemetery, Jefferson City
METZGER, Marlin D.	Cpl	374th Troop CG, 6th TCS	NEBRASKA, Hillcrest Cemetery, Omaha
MONTGOMERY, Charles D.	Pvt	49th FG, 7th FS	HAWAII, National Memorial Cemetery of the Pacific, Honolulu
OGREN, Jack A. (Navigator)	2/Lt	317th Troop CG, 46th TCS	Unsure - thought to be OHIO (Army records not located)
PARKER, John W.	Pfc	809th Chemical Co	SOUTH CAROLINA
PENSKA, Frank S.	Pfc	374th Troop CG, 6th TCS	HAWAII, National Memorial Cemetery of the Pacific, Honolulu
POWELL, George N.	Maj	49th FG, HQ Sqn	VIRGINIA, Arlington National Cemetery, Fort Meyer
RUDNICK, Anthony	Sgt	565th Sig Bn, Co A	NEW JERSEY, Beverly National Cemetery, Beverly
SAMPSON, Charles W.	Cpl	8th SG, 11th SS	NEW YORK
SEIDEL, Arnold	Pfc	5th Air Force, 415th Sig Co	MINNESOTA, Fort Snelling National Cemetery, Sth Minneapolis
SKAGGS, Jacob O., Jr.	Cpl	27th DRS	OKLAHOMA
SMITH, Franklin F.	Cpl	38th BG, 405th BS	HAWAII, National Memorial Cemetery of the Pacific, Honolulu
SMITH, Raymond H.	Cpl	35th FG, 40th FS	HAWAII, National Memorial Cemetery of the Pacific, Honolulu
SWEET, Frederick C.	Pfc	481st SS, 46th Ord Co	MICHIGAN
TENNY, Edward	Cpl	479th SS	WEST VIRGINIA, Big Bend Cemetery, Upshur County
TILESTON, David E. (Radio)	Sgt	317th Troop CG, 46th TCS	HAWAII, National Memorial Cemetery of the Pacific, Honolulu
Van FOSSON, Dale	Pfc	8th SG, 1160th QM Co	WEST VIRGINIA, Grafton National Cemetery, Grafton
VAUGHN, Ruben L.	Pvt	5th FC, HQ Sqn	TEXAS
WHELCHEL, Frank E. (Crew Chief)	S/Sgt	374th Troop CG, 22nd TCS	GEORGIA, Lyons City Cemetery, Lyons
WILLIAMS, Charles M.	Pfc	455th SS	MISSOURI

 A plaque on the Bakers Creek Memorial with these names was unveiled on 14 June 1995. Annual parades are held, and Australian and U.S. Flags are flown daily, weather permitting.

Chart by Teddy W. Hanks and Colin E. Benson - 2000

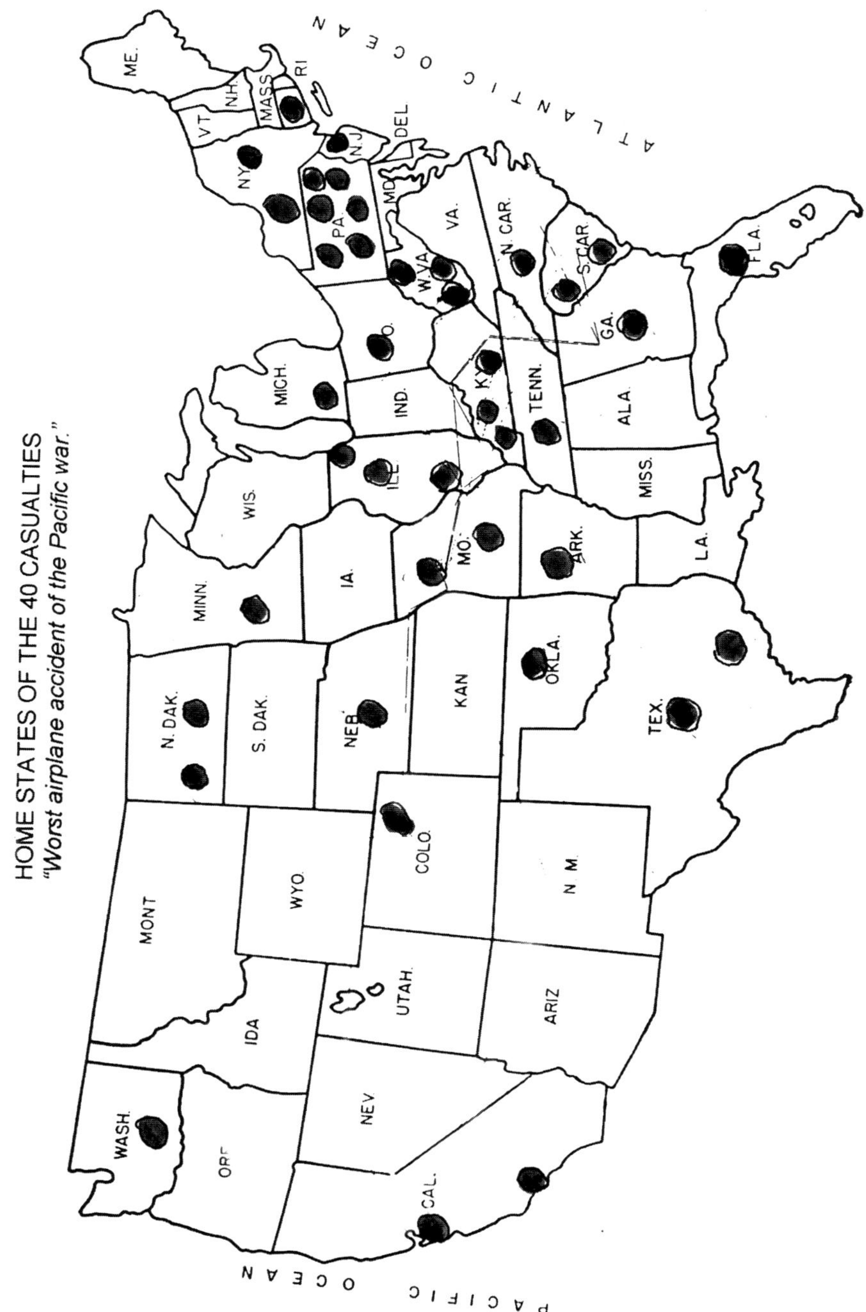

Map of United States Showing Casualties' Home States

18

The Bakers Creek Memorial

The Bakers Creek Memorial now stands as a reminder of the welcomed presence of those American servicemen who died in Mackay during the Second World War. The goodwill they left behind continues nearly sixty years later. However, the loss of the big Flying Fortress and the 40 American GIs went unheralded because of wartime news restrictions.

In 1983, Rodney Manning, then editor of *The Daily Mercury*, suggested that perhaps a memorial be constructed before the

WW II tragedy was completely forgotten. Several community leaders, including Edmund Casey, [12] the representative to the Queensland Parliament from the Mackay district in the 1980's, joined the Bakers Creek Memorial Committee. They both had grown up in the Mackay area with knowledge of the horrible wartime crash. They remembered that, as young boys, the military police had been kept them away from the crash site, days after the crash occurred.

Eventually the concept of a permanent memorial became a reality. It was proposed to the President of the Mackay-Sub Branch of the Returned Services League (RSL), in late 1991, to also mark the forthcoming 50th Anniversary of the WW II Flying Fortress crash in June 1993. A committee of local citizens was formed and a suitable site chosen about a mile from the crash site, next to the Bakers Creek Community Hall. The members agreed upon a unique design featuring two brick columns supporting a large aircraft propeller. The simple brick and metal structure was soon constructed with donated materials and volunteer effort.

Courtesy Colin E. Benson

The Bakers Creek Memorial - 1996

The following year on May 11, 1992, in conjunction with the State of Queensland's 50th Anniversary celebration of the Battle of the Coral Sea, the Memorial officially was unveiled at Bakers Creek, near Mackay, and formally dedicated – *to the forty American servicemen who perished near there, and to the sole survivor.*[13]

The ceremony was attended by a large group of local citizens and by several US veterans who had served with the 46th Troop Carrier Squadron in Mackay during the Second World War.

Commemoration Ceremonies

When the Memorial was formally dedicated on May 11, 1992, there were two former members of the 46th Troop Carrier Squadron, Fifth Air Force, in attendance. Also were the commanding officer and a contingent of sailors from the US Navy ship, USS Reuben James, who were visiting Queensland for the 50th Anniversary Coral Sea celebrations. Since then, annual commemoration ceremonies have been held on or near the anniversary date of the crash.

Retired US Army Colonel Lew Millett, a Congressional Medal of Honor winner from the Korean War, was a special guest at the commemoration ceremony on May 19, 1994. And WW II veteran, MSgt. Jack Sheafe, USAF (Ret.), unveiled the full listing of the forty casualties names engraved on a bronze plaque attached to one of the Memorial's brick columns at ceremony held on May 19, 1995.[14]

In subsequent years, there was American participation at several annual ceremonies, with guest speakers in 1996, 1997, and in 1999. And in 1999, commanding officers and sailors of several US Navy ships visited the Memorial to honor the fallen American servicemen of World War II.

These ships were:

* USS Paul F. Foster (June 1999)
* USS O'Brien (September 1999)
* USS Rushmore (November 1999)
* USS Hopper (April 2000)
* USS Juneau (May 2001)

*[insert photo 34 – BCM Ceremony – June 2, 2002]

Caption:] (photo by John Pickup)

Courtesy John Pickup

Local Air Cadets cadets provide honor guard at the 10th Anniversary ceremony for Bakers Creek Memorial on June 2, 2002

A group of US Air Force veterans and family relatives of the crash victims decided in September 2000 to build a bronze, scale model replica of a B-17C Flying Fortress to donate to the Bakers Creek Memorial. They plan to unveil it in Mackay at the 60th Anniversary Commemoration ceremonies scheduled for June 14, 2003.[15]

It was hoped that this memorial replica would help to bring a solemn closure to the tragic wartime accident.

Courtesy Jennifer Treloar, Mackay

A gift to Mackay from America]

(l-r) Ed Crasey, Colin Benson, Mayor Julie Boyd and Terry Hayes receive a bronze Fortress replica from USA

19

A Simple Act of Remembrance

On June 4, 2000, 57 years after the crash, two representatives of the United States Air Force returned to Mackay to officially acknowledge the hushed-up B-17C accident in World War II.

There were two officers: Colonel Rick Lester, Air Attaché at the American States Embassy in Canberra, representing the USAF Chief-of-Staff, General Michael E. Ryan, and Colonel Timothy G. Murphy, director of operations, Fifth Air Force, from Yokota Air Base in Japan, representing Lt. General Paul V. Hester, commander of the Fifth Air Force. They placed a simple wreath of flowers, in the form of the Fifth Air Force emblem at the Bakers Creek Memorial, which is located about one kilometer from the crash site.

When US Air Force leaders first were informed of the Memorial and its annual commemoration ceremonies, they immediately decided to send personal representatives to make amends. Colonel Lester said, "The fact that war-time censorship resulted in the crash not being reported, and those families of the dead told only that their young sons died in an air crash in the Southwest Pacific, gives a hint to the extent of suffering that the families and friends must have gone through." [16]

It was particularly important that the USAF be well represented. In recent years there had been a steady growth of interest in the crash in the United States. According to Colin E. Benson, Mackay RSL Historian, "American war veterans have said they found it deeply touching that across the Pacific in Australia an annual ceremony is held to honor some World War II American servicemen at a memorial raised by local people." [17]

"No-one was more surprised to learn of the number of American servicemen killed in that WW II B-17 Flying Fortress crash in Australia, than the USAF's

Fifth Air Force," said Fifth Air Force director of operations, Colonel Timothy G. Murphy. "One of the surprising things about [this B-17C] incident is that, when we were invited to attend this Commemoration, we found nothing to refer to about this WW II disaster in our History Office."

Col. Murphy went on to say, "One reason we were given the opportunity to come to Mackay, and pay tribute to the forty men who perished here, is because of the compassionate people of Mackay who still remember them."

At the June 4, 2002 Commemoration parade and ceremony was also the only surviving Victoria Cross winner from the Vietnam War, Keith Payne, who holds high American honors for his bravery. And sprinkled through the crowd were other local dignitaries and people with personal links to the crash. The parade commander was Lt Colonel Brian Cutriss RFD (RL) and the Master of Ceremonies was Flt Lt Greg Williamson.[18]

Mayor Julie Boyd spoke, and the parliamentary member for Mackay, Tim Mulherin, MP, was among the wreath layers. The Reverend Jim Brown, of the Presbyterian Church of Queensland, gave a Bible reading and prayer.

Other speakers were: Ms. Joan Moodie, a former Bakers Creek resident whose parents aided Cpl. Foye K. Roberts, the crash survivor, and former 46th TCS crew chief, Delmer Sparrowe, whose life was spared by the toss-of-a-coin. Retired USAF Air Commando, Lt. Colonel Eugene Rossel, from Chino, California, also attended.

The band from the Dundula State School, which incorporated the Bakers Creek Memorial symbol into its emblem, and the Mackay District Pipe Band, played for the gathering. Both the American and the Australian national anthems were sung by those assembled. And at the conclusion, a young bugler sounded the *Last Post*.[19]

20

Letters to Family Relatives

Because of wartime security, news of the crash was not shared with the forty American families whose sons had died tragically in WWII on Australian soil. And even more disturbing, nearly sixty years later, few of those families had heard anything more.[20]

The telegram sent from the Army Adjutant General to each of the crash victims' families stated only that the loved one was killed on June 14, 1943 in the Southwest Pacific Area, and that a letter would follow. The letter, signed by a Chaplain, offered selected scriptures from the Bible, suggested other readings that might console the bereaved next-of-kin, but provided no details of the circumstances of their loss.

The only clue to the specific location of the loss was the APO number (abbreviation for Army Post Office) indicated in the return address. It was APO 922, Townsville, Queensland, Australia. And it was in the Townville's Belgian Gardens Cemetery that the forty US servicemen were buried temporarily the afternoon of June 18, 1943.

In 1992, retired CMSgt. Teddy W. Hanks read an article in his local newspaper in Wichita Fall, Texas, about Foye Kenneth Roberts and the Bakers Creek Memorial in Australia. He then realized the article was about the same airplane crash in WW II in which four of his friends perished. There was no listing of the casualties. Hanks wanted to honor his WW II buddies and those who died with them. With little to go on, it took him three years of extensive research before he was able to compile a list of casualties, because only a few were from the same unit. He then sent the list of names to the Bakers Creek Memorial.

Over the next few years, CMSgt. Hanks was able to contact over a dozen family relatives of the lost men across the United States. He wanted to share details with them about the Flying Fortress air crash and information on the Bakers Creek Memorial in Australia. More recently, the Fifth Air Force headquarters in Japan requested the official US Army Deceased Personnel Record files (IDPF) for the remaining crash victims, in order to aid Ted Hanks and others in the search for additional living family relatives.

Official Sympathy Letters

On Veterans Day, November 11, 2000, as Americans were recalling the tragedy of past wars, Lt. General Paul V. Hester, commander of the US Fifth Air Force, was busy signing "Letters of Remembrance" to relatives of several servicemen who perished in the tragic World War II aviation accident. In 1943, the Fifth Air Force had been responsible for operating the B-17C Flying Fortress (VH-CBA) that crashed near Mackay, Queensland, taking the forty lives.

General Hester expressed the compassion of the men and women of his current organization, supporting the efforts of Ted Hanks, Colin Benson and the citizens of Mackay, who still remember "the forty men of the Fifth Air Force of yesterday." [21]

He wrote:

> These men died not on the front lines, nor in the jungles of New Guinea, but nevertheless in service to their nation. They deserve to be remembered.

Many military service veterans believe the Bakers Creek Memorial is unique. Retired Lt/Col Eugene D. Rossel, representing the Air Commandos Association, from Chino, California, remarked "there are few places outside the USA where locals have built and actively maintain a memorial to US servicemen of World War II." Regarding the participation of the two USAF colonels, he went on to say, "It's never too late for a nation to show its gratitude to its service men and women, and to comfort their families for their deep loss." [22]

It is, indeed, commendable that USAF leaders have finally acknowledged this tragic wartime aviation accident. Not only is the forgotten World War II story finally known, but also there is recognition in the United States that a permanent memorial to America's loss now stands at Bakers Creek in Australia.

Fate of the Survivor

The sole survivor, Corporal Foye Kenneth Roberts, suffered major injuries in the crash, but returned to duty for the remainder of the war. In 1945, he married his Australian wife, Vera, in Sydney and left for the United States to raise a family.

Foye Kenneth Roberts (1997)

In December 2000, Col. Timothy G. Murphy, one of the officers who placed the Fifth Air Force wreath at the Memorial, sent a special letter of tribute to Foye K. Roberts and his family. And more recently, on January 21, 2003, nearly sixty years after the WW II incident and following decades of declining health, he celebrated his 82nd birthday in a Wichita Falls, Texas, nursing home, but was unable to communicate.

This brings us to the end of our story. But let us now remember the commemoration ceremony of June 4 2000.

21

Father Murf's Benediction

[Remarks by Colonel Timothy G. Murphy, Fifth Air Force, Bakers Creek Memorial Commemoration — June 4, 2000]

> *We are here to honor the memory of forty fallen Americans. And I am here to thank the people of Mackay and Bakers Creek for preserving their memory for so many years.*
>
> *As I corresponded with Col Benson, Gene Rossel and Bob Cutler in preparation for my visit, I became aware of three sets of heroes. I want briefly to honor each this afternoon.*
>
> *The first was B-17C aircraft number 40-2072. Those of you who fly or maintain an aircraft understand the close relationship that develops between an airplane and those who fly and maintain them. It causes us to name them and to speak of them in rather personal terms. Let me tell you, although B-17C "40-2072" had too short a life, this was a special lady!*
>
> *She endured the Japanese attack on Clark Air Base in the Philippines on December 8, 1941. And was one of the three B17 bombers to survive, the only one to fly again in combat.*
>
> *She was one of two bombers that endured a 40-minute attack by at least ten Japanese fighters on Christmas Day, 1941. Both she and her crew survived. She suffered severe wounds that would end her bomber career. Her crew received multiple decorations for "Valor in Action," and that is still remembered in my Air Force's history.*
>
> *She recovered to a second life as a transport and participated in the operation that stemmed the Japanese tide in New Guinea and the invasion threat to Australia. This action included the unique airlifting of soldiers, from both*

of our nations, over the high Owen-Stanley Mountains; still one of history's earliest examples of combat airlift.

War wounds, time and technology conspired to remove her from the front line of combat action in the Pacific, her short life ended here on June 14, 1943. But even to the end, she did her duty. She was indeed a hero!

The second set of heroes are those we are here to remember today -- the forty of my countrymen who died here so long ago, and Corporal Foye K. Roberts, the one whom God spared.

The list of names is profoundly moving for me. It includes some men from the 5th Fighter Command headquarters, a part of USAF's 5th Air Force where I now serve. And also men from the 374th Troop Carrier Group, the forerunner of the 374th Airlift Wing, now based at Yokota Air Base, Japan; host of Fifth Air Force Headquarters.

It includes men from the 35th Fighter Group, now the 35th Fighter Wing, which has a wonderful and rich history of service in the Pacific, and now is located at Misawa Air Base, Japan, flying the F-16. And men from the 7th and 8th Fighter Squadron, two of my nation's most prestigious units, still active and flying the F-117 Stealth Fighter in New Mexico.

The casualty list includes: officers and enlisted men, pilots and gunners, crew chiefs and radiomen, quartermasters and cooks. All were asked to answer their nation's call to arms, though poorly equipped and with little training. And they did so without hesitation.

Forty died here doing their duty, but their sacrifice was not in vain. For, joined by millions of others from both our nations, we prevailed; primarily because ordinary men like these did their duty. They were heroes!

And as I pondered their final hours of life, I discovered a third set of heroes. In our Air Force, we can draw some comfort in the knowledge that their final memories were of the natural beauty of Northeast Australia's coast, and of the overwhelming hospitality of her people.

Of course I have no personal knowledge of what they actually experienced here. But I took the opportunity yesterday to roam around a little and get a feel for what they may have seen and experienced in their final days. This small insight, coupled with having received your hospitality these past few days, and having watched your dedication to the memory of those of my country who died here, makes me feel confident they died with happy memories of the "Queenslanders of Mackay."

They were, and you are too -- heroes all!

Thanks for including the Fifth Air Force in this year's memorial service.

Thank you for remembering those who gave all. [23]

Courtesy Colin E. Benson

A Simple Act of Remembrance
Representatives of the US Air Force, Col. Timothy G. Murphy and Col. Rick Lester, US Air Attaché at American Embassy, join with Australian military honor guards and Mackay residents to remember the B-17C Flying Fortress that crashed at Bakers Creek in World War II.

Endnotes

1. Harry Moore, editorial, "We Share Their Grief," *The Daily Mercury*, 15 June 1943.

   Except for a brief ambulance notice about an injured American visitor at Bakers Creek, nothing else appeared in the press. However, the local citizens soon knew of the tragedy and waited anxiously for details. Apart from a brief report of the crash in *The Daily Mercury,* 23 August 1945, after wartime censorship was lifted, no additional details about the crash were released to the public during the early postwar years.

2. George C. Kenney, *General Kenney Reports*, 124.

3. Jess Roger, "Earth-Shuddering Crash Signaled Plane Tragedy," *The Daily Mercury*, May 11, 1992, p.4

4. Colin E. Benson, email message to R. Cutler, June 7, 2000.

5. *Ibid*

6. Delmer Sparrowe, Email message to R. Cutler, Feb. 12, 2001.

7. Terrence P. Hayes is a Mackay journalist and historian who researches and writes local history articles for *The Daily Mercury*. As a young man, he visited the crash site on bicycle and grew up in the area knowing personally about the Flying Fortress aviation tragedy in WW II. Over the years, he has penned many articles about the Bakers Creek air crash. In January 2000, he complied the Mercury's "100 Years in 100 Days," an historic record of Mackay's history to celebrate the Millennium.

8. Bruce Litte, email message to author, April 11, 2003.

9. Teddy W. Hanks, a retired USAF Chief Master Sergeant, served in World War II with the 40th Fighter Squadron in New Guinea. He lost four members of his unit in the crash of B-17C (VH-CBA) at Bakers Creek. [Letter to R. Cutler, February 5, 2001.]

10. *Ibid*

11. National Archives, letter to T. Hanks, November 17, 1995.

12. Edmund Casey was a former state politician who represented the Mackay Distract in the Queensland Parliament. As a young boy, he was early on the Flying Fortress crash scene. His father's construction company built the cattle-yards for the Borthwicks Abattoir (slaughter house) that has been on the property since the late 1950s. In the late 1970s, he tried to obtain official information about the B-17C crash from the United States government.

In 1976, he wrote to the US Consul in Brisbane for information and the names of those American servicemen killed in 1943 for inclusion in a memorial to be erected in Mackay. On January 27, 1977, he received a letter from the US Embassy in Canberra, providing information from records uncovered at the Albert F. Simpson Research Center, Air Force Historical Research Agency, Maxwell AFB, Alabama. The letter confirmed the 1943 B-17C crash at Mackay, but provided only the names of five crew members who were aboard. [Letter, Major Norman G. Barfoot, Asst. Air Attache, Embassy of the United States, Canberra, Australia, to Edward Casey, M.L.A., January 27, 1977] In 1981, Ed Casey was again able to pick up the Memorial trail with the support of Mrs. Pat Kearns (Australian born widow of a 46th TCS member)and Rod Manning (Editor of *The Daily Mercury,* and a lifelong friend). He became one of the strongest supporters for building the permanent memorial at Bakers Creek and worked with the Bakers Creek Air Crash Memorial Committee to achieve that end in May 1992.

13. Memorial Program, The Bakers Creek Memorial, May 11, 1992.

14. Colin E. Benson, email message to R. Cutler, June 7, 2000.

> At the time of the Memorial dedication on May 11, 1992, only the names of six crewmembers and the sole survivor were known. However, using the results of Teddy W. Hanks research in the United States, a plaque with forty names was unveiled at the Memorial on May 19, 1995. The listing of casualties was later confirmed from a copy of the official aircraft manifest found among records of Capt. Samuel Cutler, executive officer of the US Army Rest Area in 1943, and brought to Mackay in August 1999.

15. "Group Plans Fortress Replica," *The Daily Mercury*, Nov. 15, 2000.

16. Col. Rick Lester, remarks at RSL banquet, June 3, 2000.

17. Colin E. Benson, email to R. Cutler, June 7, 2000.

18. *Ibid*

19. Colin E. Benson, Mackay RSL *Brumbeat*, May-June 2000.

20. Honorable Gary G. Miller, "Tribute to Late Servicemen of USAAF B-17," *Congressional Record*, June 30, 2000, 1183.

21. Lt. Gen. Paul V. Hester, letters of remembrance, Nov. 11, 2000.

> Formal letters were mailed to 13 family relatives of crash victims expressing the sympathy of the men and women of the Fifth Air Force and advising them the names of their loved ones are honored at the Bakers Creek Memorial in Australia.

22. Lt. Col. Eugene D. Rossel, RSL banquet, June 3, 2000.

23. Colonel Timothy G. Murphy, remarks at the commemoration ceremony, Bakers Creek Memorial, June 4, 2000.

Appendix

Courtesy Jennifer treloar

June 14 2001

Courtesy Jennifer Treloar

A Salute of Gratitude

Bakers Creek Memorial – 10th Anniversary
June 2, 2002

Courtesy Jennifer Treloar

Mackay's Flying Fortress Bronze Replica
(l-r) Ed Casey, Colin Benson, David DeBruin, Mayor Julie Boyd, Terry Hayes
January 11, 2003

Courtesy John Pickup

Del Sparrowe and Mikey Johnson unveil their Bronze B-17C Replica

Bakers Creek Memorial
Mackay, Queensland

Mackay Air Cadet Squadron honor Guards at Bakers Creek Memorial
June 2, 2007

Riddle of the ring has a happy ending

The Sunday Mail, 12th October 2003, p.39., Brisbane, Queensland, Australia.

CRASHED: A US Air Force B-17C Flying Fortress

A WOMAN who found a dead American soldier's ring among the debris of Australia's worst plane crash has returned it to his family, 60 years later.

Mavis Doolan, 71, was just 11 when she spotted the gold high school ring in mud near the wreckage of a US Air Force B-17C Flying Fortress near Mackay, in north Queensland.

The bomber, being used as a transport, had crashed six months earlier while carrying soldiers to Papua New Guinea, killing 40 people.

At the time it was the world's worst air crash but details were suppressed by the US Government, with many relatives finding out about it only in recent years.

Families of 21 victims have still to be located, while others were told at the time their loved ones were killed in action somewhere in the southwest Pacific.

After finding the ring, which carried the words "Altoona High School" and the year 1933, young Mavis showed it to her mother.

"My mother said, 'I don't want you to give the ring to anyone until you find the rightful owners'," Mrs Doolan said this week.

But the task was almost impossible for a child in remote 1940s Australia, especially since the crash was covered up and no names were released.

Overseas phone calls were expensive, research facilities limited and the post unreliable.

So Mrs Doolan kept the ring safe in a jewellery box in her top drawer while she was busy raising her family.

"I looked at it quite often, I had an attachment to the ring," she said.

When Mackay historian Colin Benson started looking into the crash, Mrs Doolan told him about her find. Mr Benson traced the ring to a Pennsylvania high school, where assistant principal Terry Iannuzzi realised it belonged to his uncle, Alfred Frezza.

Mrs Doolan sent the ring to the US in the care of Mr Benson, who presented it to Mr Frezza's family late last month.

OWNER: Alfred Frezza

Courtesy *The Sunday Mail*

Photo by Col Benson

Mavis Doolan in Mackay gives ring to Amy Sirk from America

Frezza family welcomes return of Alfred's ring
Altoona, Pennsylvania - Sept. 21, 2003

The Washington Post

Tuesday, June 15, 2004

Victims of Long-Hidden Crash Honored

Families Finally Learning of WWII Accident in Australia That Killed 40 Servicemen

By Arielle Levin Becker
Washington Post Staff Writer

For most of her life, 54-year-old Becky Hilsheimer thought her uncle William had died of a heart attack aboard a plane during World War II. Only recently did the Arlington resident learn the truth—that her uncle and 39 other U.S. soldiers and airmen were killed when their plane crashed.

Wayne Ogren, 72, of Bremen, Ga., found out in December that his brother Jack had died in the B-17C crash in Bakers Creek, Australia, and that he had been memorialized for several years in a monument near the site. His brother was an Ohio native, and Ogren sent a Buckeye flag to Australia in March so it could be flown at the monument.

Jo Morris, 82, of Collins, Ga., had long known that her brother, Frank Whelchel, died in the World War II accident—her husband, who was also in the service, had been waiting for the plane at an airstrip before it went down in the fog. But until recently, Morris did not realize how many others had died.

Hilsheimer, Ogren and Morris, and scores of others across the country, share a new connection through the crash on June 14, 1943, a disaster that was not officially acknowledged by the Air Force until four years ago.

Yesterday, the 61st anniversary of the accident, the victims were commemorated for the first time on American soil. Family members, representatives of the Australian Embassy and the man who has helped bring the surviving relatives together, Robert Cutler of Potomac, joined in a wreath-laying at the National World War II Memorial and expressed hope that the event would become more widely known in the United States.

Though many of the victims' relatives could not attend the ceremony, several said that the recent revelations about the crash, and the overdue commemoration, have brought new clarity to the victims' legacy.

"From the information we've gotten, it has been very heartwarming and comforting to know that after all these years there have been people working on this," Morris said. "Until now," she said of the victims, "they've gone unrecognized."

PHOTOS BY GERALD MARTINEAU—THE WASHINGTON POST

U.S. veteran Carlos Dannacher, left, and John Miklavcic, a squadron leader with the Royal Australian Air Force, pause by a wreath placed at the National World War II Memorial in honor of the Bakers Creek crash victims.

Miklavcic, left, Robert Cutler and Michael J. Baier pause by the wreath they placed at the World War II memorial. Many families only recently learned about the crash.

Victims' Families Sought

Robert Cutler and other researchers are looking for the families of the following crash victims:

Pfc. Jerome Abraham, Florida
Tech. 5 William A. Briggs, South Carolina
Sgt. Carl A. Cunningham, Arkansas
Tech. 5 George A. Ehrmann, California
Flight Officer William C. Erb, California
Pfc. Norman J. Goetz, Illinois
Pfc. Vernon Johnson, New Jersey
Staff Sgt. Charlie O. LaRue, Texas
Pvt. Raymond D. Longabaugh, Kentucky
Pfc. Frank Penksa, Pennsylvania
Cpl. Charles W. Sampson, New York
Cpl. Franklin F. Smith, North Carolina
Cpl. Raymond H. Smith, Pennsylvania
Pfc. Frederick C. Sweet, Michigan
Cpl. Edward Tenny, West Virginia

Photo by Gerald Martineau – *The Washington Post*

From left, Royal Australian Air Force squadron leader John Miklavcic, Robert Cutler, Michael J. Baier and Charles K. Gailey commemorate victims of a U.S. military plane crash in Australia in 1943.

Major General Robert H. Appleby, US Army (Ret.) and H.E. Peter Baxter, Chargé d'Affaires, Embassy of Australia, place a floral wreath at the National World War II Memorial, Washington DC
June 14, 2005

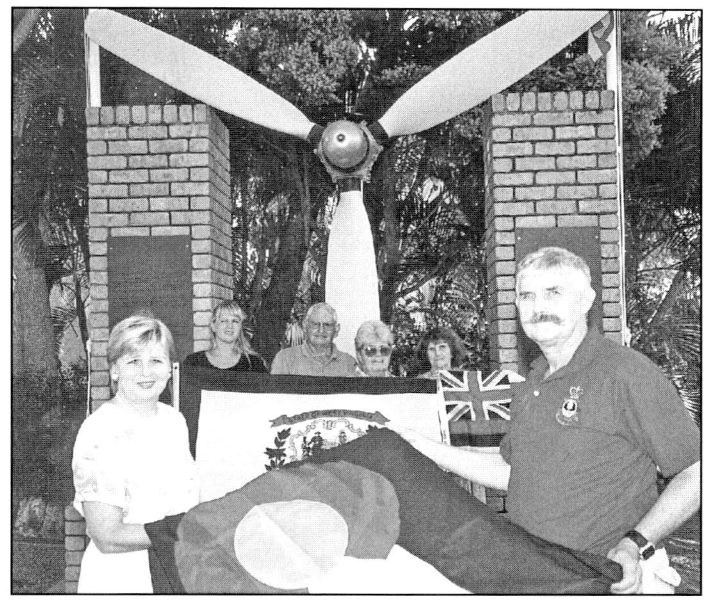

Colorado State Flag Dedication

Camille Edye, Pat Kearns, Mayor Julie Boyd, Sue Benson, Bob and Vivian Deakin

CLOSURE: Franklin F. Smith III only discovered this year his father died in the Flying Fortress plane crash at Bakers Creek during WWII.
Picture: JOHN GASS. 120605/206

US airman's son pays tribute at crash memorial

By JULIA PHIPPS
jphipps@dailymercury.com.au

IN the USA 62 years ago, 13-year-old Franklin F. Smith III was told his father died in a plane crash en route from Townsville to Hawaii.

He now knows that was not the truth.

His father, Franklin F. Smith Jr, was one of the 40 people killed in the devastating Flying Fortress crash at Bakers Creek on June 15, 1943.

A handful of US researchers, working with the Bakers Creek Memorial Committee, tracked him down in January and told him his father was in the plane crash that has been blanketed by WWII censorship for more than half a century.

Mr Smith, of South Carolina, decided immediately he wanted to visit Bakers Creek.

"About two to three months after the telegram came, they told us Daddy had taken off from Townsville on his way back to Hawaii and there was engine failure and they ran into a mountain," he said.

Yesterday he with his wife, Dot, son Franklin F. "Butch" Smith IV, and daughter Kelly Sellers attended the 62nd anniversary service of the crash at the Bakers Creek memorial.

"I was highly impressed with the monuments in relation to my father, it's been fantastic," Mr Smith said.

"I wish Americans could see what Australia has done — it's phenomenal."

The Flying Fortress took off from Mackay Airport and less than two minutes later, as it tried to return to the airstrip, it crashed where Borthwicks and Sons is now located.

Yesterday morning Mr Smith, committee members and relatives of other victims, gathered at the crash site.

"It ran chills up and down my spine and was quite a shock," he said.

"It was very, very touching.

"It gives me some closure I haven't had in all these years."

Mr Smith is a retired sale representative and now enjoys hunting, fishing and a machine workshop at his home.

At 75 he recently sold his motorcycle, but is training to re-gain his pilot's licence.

Bakers Creek Memorial Committee chairman Col Benson said within a few weeks of the initial contact, Mr Smith had phoned to ask how to get to Mackay.

Also among the 100 people at yesterday's ceremony was Jack D. Ogren, of New Hampshire, who was named after his uncle, Jack A. Ogren — the plane's navigator.

❑ **More pictures page 11.**

Family Relatives and Local Dignitaries at Bakers Creek Memorial Ceremony
Mayor Julie Boyd, BG Bradley Baker, Vice Commander, US Fifth Air Force, Hon. Santo Santoro, Franklin F. Smith III, Jack D. Ogren, and Keith Payne, V.C.
June 3, 2005

Photo by Col Benson

Pipers lead Ceremonial Parade.

Dundula State School Band
June 14, 2005

Published daily, Monday through Saturday by the Times and News Publishing Company

WEDNESDAY, MAY 31, 2006

WWII monument unveiled, ending 63 years of secrecy

BY JOHN MESSEDER
Times Staff Writer

On June 14, 1943, the *Gettysburg Times* did not report the deaths of 40 U.S. soldiers, including six Pennsylvanians, killed in a crash in Queensland, Australia. The U.S. Army would not release that information for more than a half-century, and then only under the prodding of a group of individuals spurred on by an aging veteran's diary.

"We assumed you knew," Mayor Julie Boyd said Tuesday.

The mayor of Mackay, Queensland, Australia, visited Gettysburg for a first look at a monument to the crash that took place near her town 63 years ago. Mackay had erected a similar monument in 1992 — not because the residents did not know about the crash, but because some of them finally decided the worst crash in their nation's history deserved a monument.

"They were using it in a time of need," Boyd said of the converted bomber. "It was a way to get soldiers from the battlefield for a week of R&R."

The aircraft, due for retirement, according to research by Robert S. Cutler of Orrtanna and Washington, D.C., had been rebuilt with spare parts, and pressed into service ferrying soldiers from the battlefields of New Guinea to week-long bouts of rest and relaxation in Australia.

On June 14, 1943, Flying Fortress number 40-2072, experienced problems which research not undertaken until years later could only surmise. The pilot attempted to return to the Bakers Creek aerodrome, but instead the plane crashed, killing all by one.

(See MONUMENT, Page A8)

JOHN ARMSTRONG/GETTYSBURG TIMES

Mackay, Queensland, Australia Mayor Julie Boyd and Gettysburg Mayor William Troxell trade national flags and a key to Gettysburg in front of a memorial to the victims of a B-17 crash near Mackay on June 14, 1943. The monument, which supporters hope will be placed in Arlington National Cemetery, depicts on its front the Flying Fortress and a short paragraph explaining the event, and on the rear a list of the 40 U.S. soldiers who died in what remains the worst aviation crash in Australian history.

Monument

(Continued from Page A1)

But in the U.S., the soldiers families were told only that their men had lost their lives somewhere in the Pacific theater. The secret, initially probably to prevent the Japanese from using the information as propaganda, was mostly likely made permanent in a quagmire of post-war bureaucracy.

Until, in 1989, Cutler found his father's WWII diary while preparing to move the elderly gentleman to a nursing home. The diary confirmed a story to which former U.S. Army Capt. Samuel L. Cutler had only alluded.

Capt. Cutler, it turned out, had been the Officer of the Day who loaded the 41 soldiers on the plane. In his diary, his son also found the original manifest, containing the names of all on board.

The story set in motion efforts to find the soldiers' families — 37 so far have been located — and erect a monument to the men similar to the one in Australia.

The monument's body is a gray granite slab engraved on its front with an illustration of the B-17 bomber, and on the rear with the emblem of the Fifth Air Force, of which the 46th Troop Carrier Squadron, which flew the air transport planes, was part.

On the front, a bronze plaque describes the "worst accident involving a transport aircraft in the southwest pacific during World War II."

A bronze panel on the back lists the six crewmembers and 35 passengers, including the lone survivor, Capt. Foye K. Roberts, of Texas.

The bronze panels are identical to those on the Mackay monument.

"Those 41 names all have families," Cutler said Tuesday. "Thirty-seven of those families know about it."

The gray granite body will rest on a base of pink granite donated by Queensland, Australia, indicating the strong ties between the two nations.

"I just think this is fantastic, bringing this back after so many years," Gettysburg Mayor William Troxell said Tuesday. "It's a wonderful thing to do."

In an informal ceremony held at Codori Memorials, Troxell presented a key to the borough to Mayor Boyd. The two also traded national flags.

An Act of Congress has given the Army responsibility for the monument's final placement, which supporters hope will be in Arlington National Cemetery. The exact location has not yet been determined.

"Now we have a concrete — literally, granite — marker that says it happened." Cutler remarked.

An official unveiling will be held June 14 in front of the World War II memorial, in Washington, D.C. About 35 members of the victims' families are expected to attend the ceremony.

The monument then will be taken to the Australian embassy, where it will await transportation to its final home.

Readers may contact John Messeder at johnm@gburgtimes.com

Courtesy *Gettysburg Times*

Casualty Family members at Bakers Creek Air Crash Marker Unveiling Ceremony
National World War II Memorial, Washington DC
June 14, 2006

Photo by Beth Cutler Szczybor

(l-r, front row) MG. Robert H. Appleby, Jane Kuchefski, Marilyn R. Fields, Becky Hilsheimer, Caty Ray, Kathryn McCaleb, Rosey Bagby, Peggy Marshall, Virginia M. Marshall, Wilma Post, and Carol Hadlock.
(back row) Peter Tileston, Belinda Green, Carla Ray, James Szczybor, Randy Fields, MSgt. Mark Elrod, Frank Morris, Frank Smith, Franklin F. Smith III, Wayne Ogren, Franklin F. Smith IV, Cheryl Ranwez.

Courtesy *Embassy of Australia*

Embassy of Australia Defence Staff at National World War II Memorial
Washington DC - June 14, 2006

Dedication Ceremony
Selfridge Gate to Arlington National Ceremony at Fort Myer
Washington DC — June 11, 2009

Photo by Ron Harris

USAF Lt. Gen Bruce A. Wright (Ret.) AVM Kim Osley, Head, Embassy Defence Staff, Secretary of the Army, Pete Garen, Harry McAlpine, President, RSL Washington Sub-Branch, COL Laura J. Richardson, Commander, Ft. Myer Garrison, Robert S. Cutler, BCMA (USA), David Stuart, Deputy Chief of Mission, Embassy of Australia.

Hon. Santo Santoro indicates Pedestal of Queensland Pink Granite

Photo by Ron Harris

Relatives of Bakers Creek Air Crash casualties gather at Dedication Ceremony
Selfridge Gate to Arlington National Cemetery
Fort Myer, Virginia
June 11, 2009

Photo by Ron Harris

Bakers Creek Air Crash Memorial Dedication Ceremony
(Rear view of Marker)

Courtesy PACAF Photo

Major General Jay Raymond (center), Vice Commander, US Fifth Air Force, poses for picture with Royal Australian Air Force leaders and members of Bakers Creek Memorial Committee.
June 3, 2012

Bakers Creek Memorial at Mackay
70th Anniversary Commemoration Ceremony
June 2, 2013

Ambassador Kim Beazley and Col Carl R. Coffman, Garrison Commander, Joint Base Myer-Henderson Hall, pay tribute at Wreath Ceremony
June 14, 2012

Hon. Santo Santoro, Ambassador Kim Beazley, and Col Fern O. Sumpter, Garrison Commander, with Casualty Family members at 70th Anniversary Commemoration Ceremony in Washington DC.
June 14, 2013

Bakers Creek Memorial
Mackay, Qld Australia

Bakers Creek Air Crash Monument
Selfridge Gate to Arlington National Cemetery at Fort Myer
Washington, DC.

Bibliography

1. James D. Rorrison, *Nor The Years Contemn: Air War on the Australian Front, 1941-42,* Brisbane: Palomar Publications, 1992.

2. Christopher F. Shores and Brian Cull with Yasuho Izawa, *Bloody Shambles*, (Volume 1), London: Grub Street, 1992.

3. William L. White, *Queens Die Proudly*, New York: Harcourt, Brace & Company, 1943.

4. Philip McKee, *Warriors With Wings*, New York: Thomas Y. Crowell Company, 1947. p 27-40.

5. Walter D. Edmonds, *They Fought With What They Had: The Story of the Army Air Forces in the Southwest Pacific*, 1941- 1942, Boston: Little, Brown and Company, 1951.

6. Herbert S. Brownstein, *The Swoose: Odyssey of a B-17,* Washington: Smithsonian Institution Press, 1993.

7. George C. Kenney, *General Kenney Reports*, Office of Air Force History, Washington, DC, U.S. Air Force, 1987.

8. Michael John Claringbould, *The Forgotten Fifth*: A Photographic Chronology of the U.S. Fifth Air Force in World War Two, Second Edition, Canberra ACT, Aerothentic Publications of Australia, 1999.

9. Edward Jablonski, *Flying Fortress: The Illustrated Biography of the B-17s and the Men Who Flew Them*, Garden City, New York: Doubleday & Company, Inc., 1965.

10. Peter M. Bowers, *Fortress in the Sky*, Granada Hills, CA: Sentry Books, 1976.

11. Pat Robinson, *The Fight for New Guinea: The Story of MacArthur's First Offensive*, New York: Random House, 1943.

12. Samuel Fishbein, *Flight Management*, Westport CT: Praeger, 1995.

13. Martin Cadin, *Flying Forts*, New York: Balantine Books, 1968.

14. W.P. Craven and J.L. Cate, *The Army Air Forces in World War II*, (Vol. 2), University of Chicago Press, 1952.

15. Tom Brokaw, *The Greatest Generation*, New York: Random House, 1998.

About the Author

Robert S. Cutler is a retired engineering management professor from The George Washington University in Washington, D.C. (USA).

He earned a B.S. degree in Mechanical Engineering from the University of Massachusetts and a master's degree in Management Science from Stevens Institute of Technology. Mr. Cutler was a policy research analyst at the National Science Foundation (1973-1990) and a Fulbright Fellow at University of Tokyo (1986-1987). He wrote numerous articles in his field and edited three books: Science in Japan, (1987); Engineering in Japan, (1991); and Technology Management in Japan, (1993).

In 1977, he completed a 20-year flying career as a navigator in the US Air Force Reserve. During the Vietnam War, he served as a combat crew navigator on C-141 and C-SA transport aircraft.

In August 1999, he traveled to Australia to conduct research for a book about the US Army Air Forces in Australia during the Second World War. Material for this book was drawn from his published articles, "World War II B-17C Air Crash in Australia, Uncovered," *Air Power History* (Spring 2003) and, "The World War II Bakers Creek Air Crash," *Journal of Army History* (Summer 2010).